Roll the Stone Away

Ann Hite's *Roll the Stone Away* is an unflinching yet tender look at how her family's Georgia history has shaped her—a timely memoir for lovers of story, research, and honesty.

— Jessica Handler, author of *The Magnetic Girl* and *Invisible Sisters*

In *Roll the Stone Away*, Ann Hite journeys into her past with a pocketful of burden-shaped stones. With great courage that defied her cautious nature, she faced the demons her family had hidden for generations. In the darkness, she faced murder, racism, bigotry, and hatred, yet she found compassion for her family, herself, and a love for them and from them that she didn't realize she possessed. This is one Southern woman's story but one that is hauntingly familiar to many of us. In this telling, Hite breathes new life into future generations and brings hope to those of us who have suffered in similar ways. A brave and important work. Bravo!

—Karen Schwettman, owner of FoxTale Book Shoppe, Woodstock, Georgia

Roll the Stone Away by Ann Hite is a remarkable book. In it, Hite explores her ancestry as she traces her family's path from its arrival in Appalachia until the present. Along the way she examines the sheer weight of family—the stones—and as she reflects upon the people and places who have combined to make her who she is, she examines and then lays aside those burdens that history places upon us all. Chapter by chapter and page by page, as she rolls away her stones, she teaches us that we, too, can be free.

—Raymond L. Atkins, author of *Set List* and *South of the Etowah*

I0808961

MERCER UNIVERSITY

MERCER UNIVERSITY PRESS

Endowed by

TOM WATSON BROWN

and

THE WATSON-BROWN FOUNDATION, INC.

Roll the Stone Away

A Family's Legacy of Racism and Abuse

Ann Hite

MERCER UNIVERSITY PRESS
Macon, Georgia
2020

MUP/ P598 / P598e

© 2020 by Mercer University Press
Published by Mercer University Press
1501 Mercer University Drive
Macon, Georgia 31207
All rights reserved

25 24 23 22 21 20   9 8 7 6 5 4 3 2 1

Books published by Mercer University Press are printed on acid-free paper that meets the requirements of the American National Standard for Information Sciences—Permanence of Paper for Printed Library Materials.

Printed and bound in the United States.

This book is set in Adobe Garamond Pro.

Cover/jacket design by Burt&Burt.

Paperback ISBN   978-0-88146-732-1
eBook ISBN   978-0-88146-748-2

Cataloging-in-Publication Data is available from the Library of Congress

Dedicated to my mother in hopes I did justice to the telling of our lives.

To Ella Hite because she never knew my family: may this help clarify blurry places.

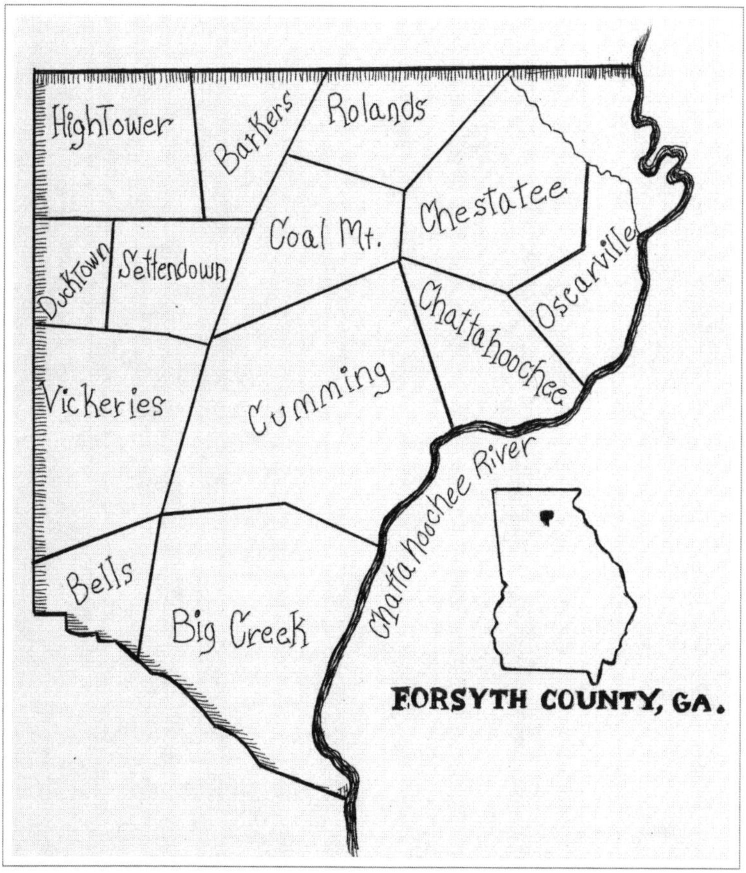

Map of Forsyth County, Georgia.

Henry Lee and Asalee Redd Hawkins
with their first three children, 1904.

Inas Hawkins and Jacob D. Lord (JD)
on their wedding day in front of courthouse,
Roswell, Georgia, March 15, 1925.

Left to right: Doris Hawkins, Audrey Hawkins (Jeanette's best friend), Corrine Hawkins, Jewel Hawkins (eldest daughter of Corrine and Ernest), Inas Hawkins Lord, and Jeanette Lord. This photo was taken during the summer of 1933, shortly after Jeanette's sister, Jeneva Estell Lord, died.

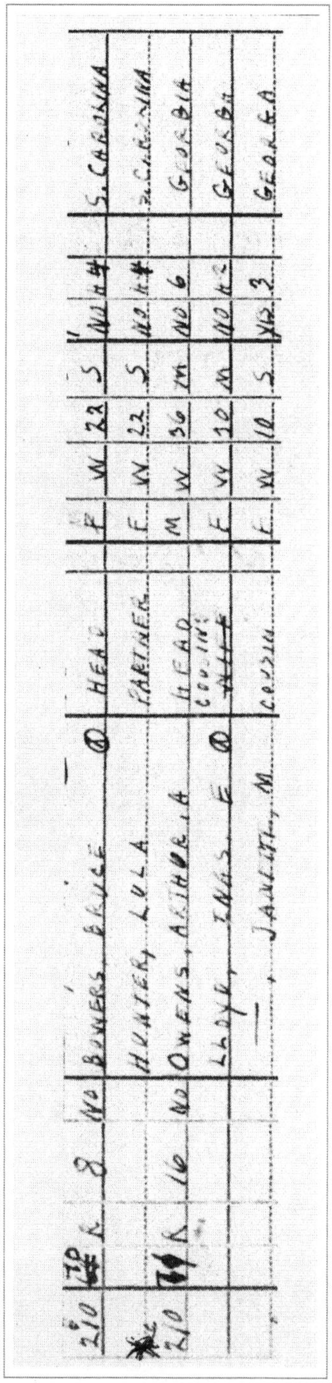

Detail from a 1940 Census page showing Inas Hawkins Lord and Arthur Owens living together in Lancaster, South Carolina.

Inas Hawkins Lord and Jeanette Lord standing in front of Ernest's old store, Newtown, Georgia, 1943.

School photo of Jeanette Lord at age 14, 1943.

Jeanette Lord (age 16) in front of Inas's house, 1945.

Jeanette Lord (age 17) with her cousins, 1946.

Ernest Hawkins, Inas's brother, the savior of the Hawkins Family, 1949.

Jeanette Lord Swafford holding Ann (age 1 week)
in Macon, Georgia, 1957.

Jeanette, Glover, and Ann Swafford at Langley Air Force Base,
Newport News, Virginia, 1960.

Glover, Jeff (age 4 months), and Ann Swafford (age 6) on picnic in Germany, May 1964. (Jeanette is the photographer.)

Ann and Jack's wedding day, May 3, 1997. Left to right: Jeanette Lord Swafford, Ann Swafford Hite, Jerry (Jack) Hite, and Ella Ruth Hite.

Roll the Stone Away

Introduction
The Story of How I Came to Own My Stones

I grew up thinking I had enough.
Enough family, enough memories, maybe too many.
I didn't need to know whose DNA I carried.
I most certainly didn't need to know their stories, secrets, lies.
Then one day I found a stone—small, smooth, ordinary.
This stone was on the grave of my grandfather, a man I never knew.
The stone was a question, proof that his grave existed, that he was once loved.
His name had never been spoken to me. Only initials. JD.
What woman forgets her husband's name when she lived with him for years before he died?
What wife has only the initials placed on his granite stone?
A woman with many secrets? Lies?
I placed the stone on my desk and began to look for answers, for family, for history.
For a legacy.

The writing of this book began long ago, while playing with my best friend Rose on the school playground when I was in the first grade on Hahn Air Force Base in Germany.* We

---

* "On March 21, 1951, 1,280 acres of land were acquired for an air base near the two small villages of Hahn and Lautzenhausen in the Hunstruck area of West Germany that the French zone acquired after WWII. The land was mostly woods and farm land in a rural area around sixty miles west of Wiesbaden. The 7356th Air Base Squadron was the first United States Air Force unit to arrive at Hahn on September 2, 1952" ("Hahn's

loved talking about our favorite dolls and playing house, pretending to be sisters with the same mom, her mom of course, not mine, never mine.

Rose didn't live in my apartment building but was close enough for the two of us to meet on one of the many playgrounds provided for all the kids on the base. The swings were the most popular. This was a time way before video games and personal computers existed. The Armed Forces TV station didn't sign on each weekday until six in the evening. And the television shows were three-year-old reruns. So kids were left to their own devices, imagination and physical play.

The swings moved high into the sky, and the bravest of the brave kids jumped to the ground, rolling down the grassy slope. My dream was to have the guts to leap from one of the swings and listen to the cheers erupting. But I could barely swing myself. My scrawny arms lacked the strength to pull the chains. Maybe it was a lack of finesse. Maybe it was just my introverted dread of others watching. Kids, waiting in line, yelled at me to pass the swing to someone else and stop trying. Rose accepted my shortcomings. Like me, she was afraid of many things—the wind blowing too hard, or the bomb drill sirens—and was over cautious.

Each afternoon, excited screams filled the playgrounds, making the detection of a parent's voice impossible. The fall air that year was the best short-sleeve weather so far on the mountain. We lived in the heart of the coldest part of Germany, complete with a small village nearby that made one think they had stepped back in time a century or two. Not one

History: The Construction of Hahn," available at http://www.hahnabk9.com/building-hahn.htm).

citizen there owned a car, only horses and wagons. The beautiful Rhine River sat in the valley below us. The place was removed from the whole world. The center of the universe. Or so I thought. On that afternoon we weren't thinking of the silent cold winter around the corner. The snowy frigid nights that forced the kids inside long before dark. The time of year when the lonely attics spanning the long apartment buildings, where the heat from the radiators settled, became our only way to move from one apartment to another. So if I wanted to visit a friend on the other side of the building, I had to go through four lengthy, extremely creepy, connecting rooms before I could emerge down the steps. Dad said my fear of the attics was nonsense. But nobody made him run the shadowy, barely lit rooms. Adults could go outside when they wanted. Yet, even if he had run the attics, he wouldn't have been frightened. He fought in two wars. Not much scared him. Rose was terrified of the attics. Her brothers, both older, on multiple occasions tortured her by hiding in the dark corners when she was forced to use this dreaded way home from an errand for her mother. Once they scared her so bad, she dropped the cup of milk her mother sent her to borrow. As I said, we were a perfect fit.

That noisy warm afternoon, I never heard Mother calling from the balcony of our apartment. This was enough to send her into a tizzy and forced her to come searching. Had she looked out my bedroom window, she would have seen Rose and me trying out Rose's new roller-skates—the metal kind that adjusted to fit over your shoes—on the grass until we could balance enough to move smoothly down the sidewalk. Both of us dreaded skinning our knees and elbows.

"Ann, it's time to come inside. I called you over and over." Mother's long shadow stretched across Rose and me, a frown slicing her forehead. At a young age, I had learned her expressions, knew what would come if I didn't act quickly.

"I'm sorry." I sat down and worked the tight skates off my brown shoes.

"Who is this?" Mother's arms were folded over her chest while she stared at Rose.

"My name is Rose. Me and Ann are best friends. We're in the same class together."

God help, Rose loved to talk. There wasn't one adult that scared her. This was the only difference we had.

"I live in building C with my two older brothers and our parents. Mama says Daddy works with Ann's dad."

Mother's cheeks tinged pink. She believed in children being seen and not heard. "Let's go, Ann."

"I'll see you tomorrow, Rose."

She nodded.

Mother and I walked in silence until we were out of Rose's hearing range. When she spoke—still looking straight ahead—her voice could have formed icicles in the warm air. "You can't be friends with that nigger girl."

Mother had never said this word around me and certainly not in such a hateful tone. I had no idea what she meant. I questioned her, something I never did. "What does nigger mean?" I said this loud enough to make a mother on her balcony turn to look.

Mother reached down and pinched the tender skin inside my arm. "My daughter will not be wallowing all over a black girl."

I turned to look back at Rose as she sat on the grass putting on her skates. Her skin was brown, beautiful. "But she's brown, not black, so that's okay."

Pain seared through my arm as Mother dug her perfectly kept nails deeper into my skin. "Do I need to give you a spanking with the belt when we get to the apartment?"

This silenced me. But I knew Mother was wrong. She was wrong. I had to be friends with Rose. But in those days parents weren't worried so much about their kids making friends or playing. They cared more about how kids made the parents look. Or at least mine did.

I still played with Rose at recess each day, but Mother wouldn't let me out of her sight in the afternoons.

A week went by and finally Rose questioned me at recess. "Why don't you come out to play after school anymore?"

In the sixties, six-year-olds still had most of their innocence, and that allowed them to be painfully honest. "My mother says I can't be friends with a black girl." I didn't use the bad name Mother had said. Something deep inside told me it was a hurtful word way before Daddy told me such a word shouldn't come out of anyone's mouth, adult or kid, and gave Mother one of his disapproving looks.

Rose's face turned into a mad frown. "You're mean and stupid." Then she stomped off and wouldn't speak to me the rest of the day.

I wanted to tell her I couldn't help what Mother thought, that I had to mind her no matter what.

The next day Rose walked up to me. "Mama said your mother is ignorant, but that I should give you a chance because you might not be stupid like her."

Mother disapproved of me as a child in so many ways, but my love was fierce. I always defended her, and this time I turned my back on Rose. Ignorant was a word I didn't know, but at the same time I understood that if I looked up the definition in Daddy's dictionary, I would find Mother's description. It was my job as her only daughter to stand up for her. I did.

On that day in September 1962, this book formed way down in my chest and began to etch words into my very upbringing. Would my family's history be my legacy?

I came into this world as a package deal. Around my neck was a sackful of stones, smooth and round like the ones Virginia Woolf used on her fateful last day as she waded into the River Ouse close to her home in Sussex, or like the perfect throwing stones used to kill Stephen in biblical times as Saul held the cloaks, or in some cases like the giant boulders growing from the rich dirt in the foothills of the Appalachian Mountains where my ancestors worked to put food on the table. The stones in my sack were so heavy that I was a late walker and a timid, sensitive child. Most of these rocks were passed on to me by family members before my mother was old enough to fall in love and marry. Some were as new as a few hours before my birth in the little hospital located at Warner Robins Air Force Base. And my coming into the world on a December morning—when a rare snow fell on Macon, Georgia—prompted more stones to be added to my soft, invisible leather pouch. Every person would like to believe they were anticipated, wanted, loved. I was told this was true of me. Yet…

The largest stone in my sack—as large as the one blocking Christ's tomb on resurrection morning—was Mother's secret, the elephant in the room we all tried to hide and deny. The best way to describe Mother is to paint an image of a hummingbird in front of a bright red flower, beating its wings against the air to stay in one place. And me, I was the chameleon, melting into my surroundings, invisible in her presence. This transparency ensured me a place in her world I both hated and loved in the same long inhalation.

My birth came in an age when women were held down, molded, crafted into carbon copies of each other. Most women married early, had children, and took care of the homes their husbands so kindly provided for them. I was born on December 9, 1957, to Jeanette Mildred (Loyd) Lord and Glover Allen Swafford. I was raised by women who were suppressed to the point they became desperate for freedom, for a different life, one they chose, in a time when history refused to grant them such a luxury. And there is always a price to be paid for going against the norm, for attempting liberty.

At the age of ten, my storytelling gene began to bloom while I sat at the knee of my granny, Inas Elene Hawkins Lord. I discovered my way into the written word by reading books with powerful characters, a habit I picked up as a child. Novels, whether they were adult or juvenile, provided me with substance. One could say they were my mentors. It was Granny who placed the first real chapter book in my hand when I was ten. *Jane Eyre.* No one told me that I was too young to grasp the true essence of this book. I read it and responded to the character of the mad wife by writing my own version of her story.

Like many from her generation, Granny used her storytelling skills to tell me and others only what she wanted us to know, so if she needed to lie a "little," she felt free to do so; after all, these truths belonged to her. Many bones are buried in her background that have been unearthed during the examination of the stones in my pouch. What she said I believed, and to this day, after unearthing many secrets—some would insist they were lies—I still find myself not questioning her version of an event until research, logic, and reason proves her wrong. In other words, until the Big Man Upstairs drops a brick on my head.

Not once while Granny was alive did she take me to visit the graves of her family members, not even my very own grandfather, whom she never called by name. So hidden was his identity, Mother did not know her father's name even though he lived with Inas and her for five years. In the 1967 South, visits to family cemeteries were an unwritten rule, faithfully obeyed by most families. Inas often broke with tradition when the results suited her cause or situation. She was a rebel, and this is something I always loved about her. When Granny died in October 1993, I still didn't know where my great-grandparents were buried. To be honest, I wasn't even curious. Our small family unit held enough history to last me a lifetime. Maybe too much. When it came to extended family, I never felt there was a thread linking me to something larger. My life had been shielded from anything and anyone outside of Granny, Mother, and Jeff, my little brother. My father had left us behind when I was still nine. I was taught to be wary of anyone who claimed some kind of kinship because they probably had a distrustful motive. Never did I feel I had missed out because I didn't have a large family tree. The four of us were enough

So how did I come to actually write this book? In 2014 I received the only known photo of Asalee Redd Hawkins and Henry Lee Hawkins, my great-grandparents, Granny's parents. I connected with Asalee immediately. Her DNA pushed through my veins. Her expression, solemn, told me she held the insight into my family if only I would listen. This sounds crazy to my dear readers, but Granny's roots were deep in the foothills of Appalachia, where folks still believe people don't begin talking loud enough to be heard until they die. Could I right/write my family's truths? The thought scared me to death. But for a writer, once a thought digs in, there is no letting go. I googled Asalee Redd Hawkins, and a link to "Billions of Graves"—a website that helps people locate graves—provided me with a cemetery name, a photo of Asalee's headstone, and a description of where the grave was located. When I realized Asalee was buried without Henry Lee, I was hooked. Henry Lee was buried in the same cemetery but as far apart as he could possibly be and still remain in the same graveyard. Asalee's plot was near the front of Friendship Baptist Cemetery with its rolling hills of gravestones dating as far back as the 1700s. I would learn later that many of these people were part of my story. So much for not having a large family tree. Henry Lee was found at the very back of this graveyard with only a tree line separating him from an old house—old enough to have been there when he was buried—decaying into ruin. Asalee's headstone was five feet tall and made of Georgia marble with tassels carved into the corners. I placed my hand on the cold marker and waited, listened to every sound around me. Did she know I was there? Was her essence somehow still around, waiting to tell the truths she couldn't tell while she was alive? What was taken from me with her early death? She died on August 5, 1915. Granny was six years old. Beside her grave were two other stones belonging to Bertha and Mary Hawkins. Bertha's marker was also tall, with Jesus hanging from the cross, and had the words "Asleep in Jesus" carved into the stone along with the dates of birth, 1907, and death, 1922. Bertha died at fifteen. Next to her was a small, plain marker—only inches tall—stating, "Mary L. Hawkins 1915-1924." The lettering was plain and simple, suggesting something had changed in the two years after Bertha's death. Mary was nine when she died. While Granny told me many stories about her family and childhood, talking about Bertha many times, never had she spoken of Mary, her youngest sister.

In spring 2012—long before I even imagined I would write this book—I was working on final edits for *The Storycatcher*, my second novel. I also had a half-finished third novel that frankly lacked a story, dead in the water, but my publisher at the time wanted to see the work as soon as I finished. My oldest daughter, Melissa—in her late thirties—called to ask me questions about Inas, her great-grandmother. She was building a family tree. Haven't we all hit this age and begun to wonder about family? But this was the type of project that could derail all my work, tempt me to drop down the research hole—a yawning opening always ready to distract me—where I often love to dwell, rather than write. I gave Melissa the answers and explained that as much as I wanted to dig into this with her, I couldn't. I was under deadline. The next day, she sent me an email. The subject read, "Missing Sister of Sweet Granny's"—Melissa's name for Inas. How could I resist? I opened the email and read that a child had been found, Inas's youngest sister Mary Alice. She had been born to Asalee and Henry Lee on February 10, 1915, almost exactly six months before Asalee would die. Mary died a couple months before her ninth birthday in 1924. Almost exactly two years after Bertha. Inas never told me about this little sister. She actually went out of her way to rearrange Stella's age—Inas's younger sister—so she fit the role of the baby on Asalee's lap when she was pushed from the car. And it worked.

For years I never questioned the timeline. But then I found out about Mary Alice, and questions whirled in my head. How can a child die and no one pass her story down through the family so she is remembered, cherished? Hadn't Inas done this for Bertha? Why not Mary Alice? This child would not leave me alone. I thought about her all the time. A writer writes to find answers to questions. I wrote Mary Alice into the flat, fast-fading third novel, where she became Mary Grace. I gave her a story, a voice, even if it wasn't close to her truth, a truth I couldn't possibly find. Or so I thought. This character addition gave the new novel a voice, and it was accepted for publication by Mercer University Press with the title *Where the Souls Go*. Three years later, while researching this book, I found most of Mary Alice's true story. I may never know her favorite color or who she loved the best, but I know how she died.

The mystery of Mary was what finally drove me to write the stories in this memoir. How could Granny eliminate a sibling from her telling? Why? Mary Hawkins seemed more like a character out of a historical novel than my great-aunt. I needed her story. I needed the story of Asalee. Did Asalee die like Granny told me, falling as she exited their Model T Ford? Who was my great-grandfather Henry Lee Hawkins?

While roaming the hilly grounds that chilly afternoon, I began to notice that many of the graves were Redds and Hawkinses. How many of these people were part of my history? This cemetery sat in the Hightower Community of Forsyth County. How had the racist history of this place affected my relatives? Too many questions. How with most family members dead would I find the truths, the stories Granny changed or didn't tell at all? Did these truths—if I discovered them—become my history? The answers were laced into the rolling hills of Appalachia. What made Granny the woman she became? Would these stories help me to understand my mother's mental illness and Granny's dull disconnect from hard situations?

Both women, Granny and Mother, made bad choices. Both, in their own ways, lost their minds. Their madness revealed itself in the familiar forms of racism, abuse—both physical and emotional—and adultery. Many readers might argue that mental illness, a disease, doesn't make a person a racist or force a person to commit adultery, but I would urge them to consider the stories passed down through these generations. Look at the history, the tellings, so many sad, twisted happenings, and even some inspirational tales too. All proving to me that bad and good occurred to create the ancestors' stories. To create who I was. Good and bad walked hand in hand. Unfortunately, mental illness is rooted in the tellings of generations.

When I decided to explore my history, I prayed I'd find some understanding of the women who raised me, a way to balance the contradictions they could be. Always be careful what you ask. You might get your prayers answered.

The Last Stone
No More Words, 1993

Granny sits propped with pillows supporting her back in a hospital bed. Her hair sticks straight out around her head, reminding me of the famous photos of Albert Einstein. Up high, behind her, push-pinned to the wall, is a fair-sized handwritten sign, all in caps: PATIENT IS BLIND.

"Who is there? Is that you, Annie?" Granny looks toward me as if she can see me clearly.

The sign's admission strikes me silent as I stand in the doorway. We—Mother, Jeff, and I—live in denial, burying ourselves in a lie, pretending Granny's eyesight is fine, but in reality she can no longer live alone.

"Is that you, Annie?"

"Yes, Mother, it is her." My mother sits in a chair dressed in one of her many pairs of polyester pants—these are yellow—and the standard white pullover cotton shirt. She stares, as if waiting for me to give a reason for my presence. The night before, I threatened over the phone to physically carry Granny to my car and take her to the emergency room. For days, she had turned down all food and was refusing to leave her bed for anything, even to use the bathroom. Granny's arthritis is so bad it causes debilitating swelling around her joints and horrible pain. Still, she has always managed to leave the bed for short distances, saying the doctor insisted that movement keeps her mobile for longer. She has banished the idea of owning a wheelchair or walker. My once regal grandmother is reduced to this trapped soul. The two of us—once so close—have stopped speaking. I broke with tradition and abandoned the urban legend written for me on a daily basis since before my birth. Just recently I left an emotionally abusive marriage of eighteen years, and while I am terrified to be on my own for the first time in my life, I want to live, be free. With this break in my story, Granny withdrew from me, accusing me of leaving my "good" husband. She can't see me as a grown, independent woman. I understand her bewilderment with my decision since Mother had always leaned on her, especially when Dad left. But I am not my mother. I am a wannabe fiction writer who works as an office manager for a local cleaning business. The title is a recent promotion. Before this I was a maid. Yes, a maid, and Granny thought I had lost my mind. Why would I give up a "good" life to clean other people's homes? This is not her idea of independence. And it's not mine either. Each night after cleaning my last house, I came home and taught myself how to use a home computer that I had purchased with money I should have saved for my three daughters' expenses. But I was determined to be something, stand on my two feet. Write books, articles, stories that others would enjoy. And make enough money to support myself and my girls. I did this.

"Who's there?" Dark shadows make half circles under Granny's eyes. Skin sags where there should be muscles in her upper arms. She wears a pea-green hospital gown. Under normal circumstances, this woman would rather die than be caught dead in such an outfit.

"I said it's Ann," Mother snaps.

Again that blank stare is pointed at me. "Annie, I want to leave here. You have to take me home. Now. Understand?" This is the granny of my childhood. "You promised me, Annie."

Yes, God, yes—the promise pulled from me the first time when I was ten, and numerous times after. The promise not to place her in a "nursing home."

"I mean it. I have to go home."

I don't point out her home is gone, taken from her by her stepsons when the last retina transplant failed. Or maybe she is speaking of Mother's home, originally her home bought when Mother was young.

Still I stand in the door, frozen in place like the child I become each time I am with her.

"Your mama is mean, Annie." She leans in my direction with her cloudy eyes seeming to watch me. Did she sense my break in confidence? Sense it like a wild animal senses the blood of its prey?

Mother releases a ragged breath. "I told you she's been like this. Nothing I do is good enough, never has been since I was a child. I've been trying to please her since I can remember." This is Mother's standard mantra whenever Granny complains about something.

A young nurse with dark red hair comes in the room, carrying a small cup of medication.

Mother's self-centeredness and lack of empathy show through at times. "She's not taking you home, Mother."

"My granddaughter is taking me home with her today." Granny speaks in her haughty voice to the nurse.

"Mrs. Lord, take your medicine." The nurse's patient tone amazes me. Granny is in meltdown mode, and if she doesn't get what she wants, the whole hospital will know.

No. No. I can't take her to my home. Packed boxes sit around my apartment for a move I will make over the upcoming weekend. No. Not this time. I can't be the person she manipulates into what she wants.

"Annie, get my things. We're leaving. I promise I won't be any trouble at your house. I promise. Your mama pinches me when I won't eat. You know about her pinches. You know the things she does, Annie."

Yes. Yes. I know all about how Mother acts. I knew this even when Granny wouldn't admit Mother beat me. She always pointed out Mother's sickness and how we had to keep it a secret, understand her actions. If others knew, she would lose my brother and me to Dad.

The nurse gives me a hard look "If you take her out of the hospital without a doctor's release, you will be prosecuted if something happens to cause her death."

Later Mother will insist the nurse never said this, and maybe this is her truth—maybe I invent the words to relieve the pain and guilt that assault me. Would that be so bad? But in my mind, this strong memory exists. It is my truth.

Instead of speaking to the nurse, instead of acknowledging how crazy my family is, how ashamed I am of being part of this family, I take a wide-tooth comb from my purse. "I'm going to comb this hair. It's a mess. You can't be yourself because I know you wouldn't let your hair go like this." I give my mother a look. How could she allow things to get this way? How can I walk away when I am needed to straighten out this situation? The comb gets stuck in the snow of white tangles.

"I need to go home," Granny whispers. "I'll die if I stay here. You promised, remember."

A strong tug in my heart catches a hard, ragged breath in my chest. The comb, finally, releases the tangles and smooths her hair. "Now, doesn't that feel better?"

"Take me home."

When I turned ten, Dad dumped our little family at Granny's house. On Thanksgiving. I cried until tears wouldn't fall anymore. Granny gathered me in her arms, sat in the swivel rocker by the floor furnace that clicked off and on, heat pushing into my face as I turned away from her neck. My legs were so long my feet touched hers, but still, she rocked me like a baby, humming, humming into the night. Her arms were my safety net.

I pull the comb through once more. "We're going to make you beautiful again," I whisper, my lips close to her ear. What kind of person refuses to grant her grandmother a desperate wish?

"Remember when I saw you for the first time after Germany? Remember how glad I was my Annie came home?" Her tone is wispy, dreamy. Her gnarled fingers, misshapen by the arthritis, still now, quiet, no longer frantic.

She is withdrawing, turning inward, leaving me. The energy draining from us. I comb all the tangles out of her hair as she stares into her dark abyss. For so long this woman has been my lifeline, my heart, and now I am turning my back on her to save my own life. How selfish am I?

I have a practical mind that does not entertain tales of ghosts or spells that Granny and her sisters talked about all the time. Practical. Sensible. I refuse to visit Granny after that horrible day when she begged to come home with me. I know she will throw another fit, demand me to take her away. I promise myself I don't have to see her again until she comes to her senses, if she ever does. And the best plans never work for me.

Jack, my boyfriend, and I have been dating for two years. We moved in together the weekend after Granny begged to come home with me. Sometimes I think maybe I didn't want to bring Granny home because her presence in our new home might cause even more stress than blending our children together. Jack has a son and I have two daughters living with me—one a teenager and one a tween. When the accusing thought enters my mind, I push it away. I didn't bring her home because I couldn't provide the healthcare she needs. But as the days turn into two weeks, my courage falters, and the self-talk turns critical. What kind of granddaughter does such a thing? One who is so terrified of her grandmother's disapproval even if it is unjust.

Jack has a history of kidney stones, and one morning before I leave for work, he has an attack. I drive him to the hospital—the same hospital—I am not thinking about Granny. He is in terrible pain. I am worried about him and drive fast. After they examine Jack, the doctor decides to use laser surgery to break up the stone, which has the diameter the same size as the end of a cigarette. I go with Jack as far as the nurses allow me. Then I wait in one of the orange plastic chairs in the hall. My stomach churns with nerves, and reading the book I have with me is near impossible. The hospital staff walks up and down the hall. A nurse enters the hall from my right, pushing a gurney. Granny lays there with her gnarled hands pulled in close to her chest. Her hair is wild again. Her eyes are wide open but vacant of any emotion, as if she is one of the haints she and her sisters spoke of when I was young.

My heart pounds blood through the thoughts in my brain. No, I can't say anything. I can't. If I say something, if I ask why she is sitting in the hall with a clipboard beside her, then I will have to hear the answer, and this nurse will know what kind of granddaughter I really am. But how can I deny her? The woman saved me from a crazy mother and a runaway father. Now I am rejecting her. Yet if I speak, she might begin begging me to take her home. In the end, I am a coward and remain silent. I hate myself for this terrible decision, and if the truth is told, I am afraid of her, of the hold she has on me. The nurse pushes Granny through two large swinging doors.

An hour later, the doctor comes to tell me that Jack will be taken to a room for release.

"The stone was broken up, but he may experience more pain when passing the larger pieces. It was a large stone. I will give you a prescription for pain pills."

Jack is alert and in no pain when I enter his room. The nurse is readying him for discharge, but they are waiting on release papers. He is on the phone with his ex-wife about his young son's concerns. I leave to give him some privacy.

While I stand in the hall, I realize Jack is on the same floor as Granny's room. Jack can't understand my not visiting her. He has a large, noisy family; they fight, but at the end of the day they always make up and stay close. My experience has been that people who have these wonderful families don't understand the struggle of the dysfunctional dance. Granny's door is open. Each measured step down the bright, clean hall brings me closer to the nightmare vision I saw downstairs. Maybe she is still out of her room. Vertigo pushes through me momentarily, but I walk again when it passes.

Granny lies in her bed surrounded by machines beeping and gurgling. Her breathing is steady and deep. With her eyes closed and her mouth slightly ajar, I wonder if this is my granny, the one who is strong, who fights against all the horrible things dropped in her lap. Her curled position suggests a vulnerability that I never thought she was capable of. I step close to the bed.

A nurse enters the room and looks at her chart. "Are you related to Mrs. Lord?"

"Yes, I'm her granddaughter." In that second, I don't care what anyone thinks. I want to be close to Granny more than anything I've ever wanted. Shame loses the battle.

"Are you Ann or Bess?" the nurse asks.

This surprises me. "I'm Ann."

The nurse smiles as she checks a machine's readings. "When she was still talking, she called out to you and Bess all day."

"I'm sorry I haven't been here. The day she was admitted, she threw a fit for me to take her home. I caused trouble being here."

The nurse shook her head. "I know all about older patients. Who is Bess?"

"Her older sister, Beatrice. She died a few years ago."

The nurse gave me a solemn look. "She talked about seeing her in the room."

Has this nurse been raised like me, to believe in the old ways? That dying people call out to the dead? A shiver runs through my bones.

"You talk to her. Just because she's withdrawn doesn't mean she can't hear." The nurse leaves the room.

I place my hand on the tissue paper skin of her arm.

She flinches, or do I imagine this? "Granny, it's me, Ann. I'm here."

Her breaths stop for a moment and then begin again.

"Look, I'm sorry I haven't come to see you before today, but you threw such a fit, and you wouldn't take no for an answer." I realize I didn't say no to her; instead, I slithered from the room without her knowing, like the snake I am.

Her fingers on her left hand flex. My fingers are like hers, long, thin, elegant. When I married my first husband, I didn't have a wedding ring. Granny passed on to me her solid yellow-gold wedding band given to her by my grandfather when they married. I treasured the meaning the ring held, but it was much too large for my skinny little finger. I wore it anyway. When I lost it in the grocery store, I searched and searched the floor. I begged the manager to move one of the fresh-food coolers to see if it rolled under. He wouldn't, insisting the space wasn't big enough.

Instead of being furious about my losing the ring, Granny reached into her jewelry box and pulled out a white-gold band that she had worn when she married her second husband. "Here, I want you to have this."

I took the ring and placed it on my finger. This one fit.

This woman curled up in the hospital bed, my granny, can't talk to me. I rub her ring finger. "Remember when I lost your first wedding ring? I hated myself. You were so understanding and forgiving." I think about the gold band, knowing it had been my grandfather's ring, not hers. What had happened to hers? Did she lose it? Did she sell it when times got hard and money was next to impossible to come by?

Granny lifts her hand into the air and back down again while her breaths grow harder.

"Listen, I want you to know I'm okay. You don't have to hold on to this world any longer, Granny. I know you don't want to be here and it's okay. I will make something of myself.

I promise. You won't have to worry. I have a good job. I write. I even have a house now. It's not mine but I love it. You can let go. I'll miss you. I understand you always loved me, and I love you more than you will ever understand. I love you, Granny." I squeeze her fingers.

A low growling comes from her. She opens her mouth and makes another gurgling sound. Is she trying to speak to me? Her arm waves in the air.

"It's okay." I take her arm and place it back on her stomach. "I know what you would say if you could. We were always like that, weren't we?" I pat her hand.

Her breath calms and her body relaxes under my touch. She hears me, understands me.

"I'll do good for you, Granny." I rub her hair.

When I leave the room, I feel like I have encountered my worst fear and conquered it. A weight falls from my chest. She heard me. She knows I love her. No matter what happened in the two years after I left my first husband, we love each other.

Jack and I go home, and he is up all night throwing up and screaming in pain. At 5:30 he finally quiets and falls asleep. I sit on the floor, leaning my back against the bed so as not to disturb him, and fall into the deep sleep of a person far too tired.

I dream that I am walking in the hall of the hospital. I stop at Granny's door. My oldest daughter, Melissa, opens it. I try to step over the threshold, and Melissa gives me a sad look.

"Mom, Granny's not here anymore. You don't have to come in."

I jump awake. Jack is still sleeping. The clock reads 6:30. I have slept an hour.

After I call in sick to work, I wake up my youngest daughter, Beth, and take her to daycare. School is out that day, and she is going on a skating field trip. Then I drive back home.

Jack meets me at the door with the phone in his hand. "Your mom needs to talk to you." His expression tells me it is bad.

"Ann, the nurse said your granny died sometime between 5:30 and 6:30 this morning. Oh God, Ann, I haven't been to see her in over a week. Will you go with me to the hospital?"

The scene in Granny's hospital room reminds me of a movie, so surreal. Her bed is flat and a sheet covers her. My hands begin to shake, and I leave. I walk out the door to the lobby. I drink a cup of black coffee. I hate coffee. Granny loved black coffee.

Granny is buried in a light purple casket with violets embossed on the sides. I never see how she looks. Something inside of me will not allow this. When it is time for the family to leave for the graveside service, I get in the backseat of Mother's car at the front of the line behind the hearse. This is where immediate family is to ride. Jeff is behind the wheel and Mother sits beside him. She turns and gives me a harsh look that tells me I am not wanted in the car. My brother is probably high. A horrible urge to open the door and walk away from both of them forever, never looking back, comes over me. Why not? The one person who held us together, who told me I needed to look after both of them, is gone. She left me. Hadn't I told her to do just that? And if I leave the car, my life will change for the better. But I've never been one to learn a lesson the easy way. I remain in the back seat, unwanted, sad…no, devastated.

When I return home after the services, I go to rest, crawling into my bed, too tired to turn off the overhead light. I close my eyes. Silence soaks into my bones. I'm still not used to the noises in the new house. I open my eyes again, not sure why. Maybe a sound or just that feeling of being watched. Granny stands over me, staring. I am dreaming. I have to be. Then she bends over the bed. When she does, she blocks out the overhead light. A small gasp escapes me, and she disappears. Gone.

Jack walks into the room. "I thought you were sleeping. Do you want the light out?"

"No. No." How do you say you saw a ghost, or haint as Granny would have said? But what I saw was Granny, not some gauzy spirit hovering overhead. She stopped in to check on me as she left the earth, moving on from a life that in so many cases knocked her to her knees. Granny, the woman who picked me up when Dad abandoned us, the woman who took care of Mother, the woman who told me the family stories and brought some of my relatives alive for me, was gone. I don't know how I will move forward, but I know I will. I promised her. And this is one promise I have to keep.

Part One

Ann

Stone 1

A Home Not Known, 1966

The flight from Frankfurt, Germany, landed—after almost nine hours—for refueling at Kennedy Airport. I sat across the aisle from two GIs going home like my family and me. One of the GIs motioned for me to look out his window. We were entering our landing pattern into New York City. I was eight—two weeks away from turning nine. My breath stuck in my chest. The plane came close as we flew over Lady Liberty, holding her lit torch, scraping the sky, welcoming us home. Her coppery green pleased me so much I laughed. I thought of the large black-and-white photo in my geography book back on base. Out the window, skyscrapers, making a semicircle of the bay shoreline, stood reflecting the afternoon light. The Empire State Building, with its needle stabbing a low cloud, created a dream quality to the whole scene. But the view outside the window was real. We were back in the United States. How many people lived in a city as big as New York? More than the population on Hahn Air Force Base, where I had attended my first day of school and remained halfway through third grade. Daddy, Master Sargent Glover Allen Swafford, had received orders a month earlier to ship into Hunter Air Force Base outside of Savannah, Georgia. And that changed everything. Mother called, Georgia, this place we were headed to, home, a place I hadn't been able to picture no matter how hard I tried. What I knew and loved, to the very bottom of my toes, were the snowy mountains where I lived in Germany, sixty miles from the Berlin Wall. I was a military brat, accustomed to bomb drills and days spent in shelters during the Cuban Missile Crisis.* Many a Sunday afternoon, I went with Daddy to the silos where the nuclear missiles were housed underground. The most exciting visits were those when the tall, slender, rocket-like weapons were brought above ground. Around our housing was the lush, thick Black Forest where I went to play with friends, praying the wild boars didn't come after us. The "States"—spoken as a reverent name—didn't appeal to me. But my feelings didn't stop our move from taking place. For better or worse, we were home. The Statue of Liberty stood tall and proud outside my window, proof.

I never stepped a foot off the plane in New York. Instead, we headed to Charleston, West Virginia. The two GIs said their goodbyes and were replaced with two nuns dressed in full habit. Nuns were a familiar, comforting sight. I struck up a conversation with the younger one and enjoyed myself. The truth is I enjoyed talking period. The young nun allowed me to play with her rosary. She showed me how to pray, reciting a line as she touched each bead. The thrill of connecting to God in a larger way than just saying made-up prayers in my head intrigued me. Before we landed, the young nun insisted I keep the rosary as my own. The gift remained with me for at least

* Hahn Air Force Base was one of the bases in West Germany that went on alert during the Cuban Missile Crisis. The alarm came at 3:30 am. All the base went on alert ready to strike East Germany. This is the closet that the United States has ever came to nuclear war. See "The Cold War…Or Why I Hated Alerts!" available at http://www.hahnabk9.com/the-cold-war.htm.

two years. One day Mother found it and tossed it in the garbage.

Finally, we landed for the last time, collected our bags, and found Dad's 1960 pea-green Plymouth Valiant sitting in the parking lot. His precious car had made a double transatlantic trip, having left Germany by ship two weeks ahead of us. The car sitting in the parking space, waiting on us, made the whole trip real, final. We were finished with Europe, finished with the life we made there. The car was a family member who had come to take us the last leg of our trip. I wished I were a turtle or crab, carrying my home on my back and never having to adjust to new places.

"Get in the back and don't start talking, Ann," Daddy barked at me. He had been mad for well over six months. The problem began the spring day in April when I told Mother about my adventure with him at a bar in Lautzenhausen, the closest German village to the base. How he kissed a woman wearing bright orange lipstick. How I begged to drive home because I was afraid he was too drunk. Mother promised she wouldn't mention our conversation with him and sent me out to play. Of course, her promise, like all her promises to come, were air.

Daddy found me on the swings. "Why did you tell, Ann?"

A hole opened in my heart that afternoon.

"Come in the house." His words were tired.

The one person I could count on to love me wanted nothing else to do with me. I had turned traitor, a snitch, a bad girl. Our relationship had changed.

So on the day when we headed out from West Virginia, I knew there was something in the air: trouble.

Mother—thirty-eight years old—climbed in the front seat

of the car with eighteen-month-old Jeff in her lap. "Glover, Ann's just excited to be back in the States." She smiled. I can't help but wonder if she was as stupid as she seemed to the changes in Daddy.

I settled into the backseat.

"We're driving as far as we can without stopping. If you have to go to the bathroom, you better go now." He frowned a warning at me in the rearview mirror. I knew better than to open my mouth.

In Germany, a foot of snow had fallen the day we left. Now I was coatless in West Virginia with the window rolled down until Mother noticed and pitched a fit, saying I would die of pneumonia.

After dark, Mother pointed to a field where a large parking lot full of cars sat facing a giant movie screen.

"What is that?" I was mesmerized.

"A drive-in movie. You sit in the car and watch it. Some of them have a playground at the foot of the screen for the kids to play on while their parents watch in the car."

"How do you hear?" I turned to watch out the back window.

"A speaker. You hang it on the open window. You get to watch two movies for what one costs." Mother gave Daddy a side look. "Maybe your father will take us while we're visiting your granny."

Daddy never answered. Back in Germany, before I went and ruined everything, he always took me to the movies on base, and we watched Perry Mason each week on our nine-inch TV. While watching this show, we found out President Kennedy had been shot. Daddy had tears in his eyes, something I wasn't accustomed to seeing.

"We have a long way to go," Mother sang out in her fake sweet voice, trying to cover the tension in the car as if she was pushing away a bad dream. "Lay down and go to sleep, Ann. You will have a long day tomorrow."

One of us had to see what was coming at us. I watched the stars out the back window. A few more hours and I would see my granny again. Was she old? The last time I had seen her I was five. Then on Thanksgiving I would meet my aunts, uncles, and cousins on Daddy's side and eat dinner at my aunt's house. Mother promised this aunt had a phone, and I could use it. Personal phones in Germany belonged to the higher-rank officers. The sound of the tires rolling over the pavement rocked me. I was going home to a place I did not know. Maybe memories would appear in my dreams.

Sometime during the night—maybe because of a dream—I woke up obsessed with Daddy disappearing. I was sure we would be riding down the highway, and poof he would evaporate, be gone forever. Vanishing out of his seat. The steering wheel left unattended. The car would run off the road, flip, and we would die. Kids could die. My friend Molly lost a sister when she jumped from a swing and hit her head on a rock. The family left Hahn early. We could all die. Daddy could die. He might ship out to the newest war I saw on TV. Mother thought this too. A place called Vietnam. When I asked him if he could die in this war, he frowned at me. "Soldiers die sometimes, but I'm not going over there yet." This answer didn't make me feel better. Maybe I could see into the future. Maybe Daddy would disappear into the new war. Maybe he would get tired of us and just leave. Hadn't he threatened this to Mother?

In the early morning, Mother shook me from a deep sleep. I was in a strange bed alone. Sometime during the night my parents got a motel room. "Go to the bathroom. We have to leave. We will be at Granny's soon."

Dawn crept across the rolling fields on both sides of the road. We had crossed the state line into Georgia, and the sunlight melted the frost balancing on the brown dead grass, making me think of Hahn in early fall. Houses in Germany were built of stucco unless the family was extremely poor. Then the house was built of wood. On this Georgia road I saw large homes here and there, all made of wood. Georgia was a strange, different land.

"All of your family lives in this state, Ann." Mother still held Jeff—now stretched out asleep—on her lap. His sweet face still sticky from a red sucker Mother gave him so he wouldn't cry and bother Daddy, who was bothered by Jeff too often. Even I knew this. Mother told me all the time that Daddy liked me more than Jeff.

"Tomorrow you meet your family," she said, sighing.

Daddy looked straight ahead, wearing what I always thought of as his soldier face.

A million questions passed through my head, but Daddy hated for me to ask questions. I prayed to God that Granny didn't live in a wooden house. That she was not poor. We—Mother, Jeff, and me—needed a bit of luck. Daddy made his own luck. He was known for that.

When Daddy turned the car down Granny's street, I held my breath.

"This is the road." Mother laughed. Jeff bobbed up and

down on her lap, picking up on Mother's excitement.

I knew the road. I remembered. All of a sudden, the memory was there. I had stayed here when Daddy left for Germany. She, my granny, stood on the front porch of a little cottage that looked like the drawings in my fairytale books. This woman, who looked similar to my memories of her, wore a light blue dress belted at the waist and low black heels as if she was going to church. Much prettier and tidier than Mother. The smile that spread across her face shooed my fears away. How long had she been waiting? Standing there watching for her daughter and grandkids to come home? Did she sense when we were close? Was she magic? When I entered the house, the scent of some delicious treat almost knocked me down.

"What's that smell?"

"Annie, that is pound cake. Would you like a slice?"

Of course I did.

Late the next morning, we headed out to Thanksgiving dinner with Daddy's family. There is no memory of spending the night at Granny's, but I'm sure we did. The drive to my aunt's wasn't terrible, only quiet, too silent. Daddy parked his car in front of the large two-story house belonging to Aunt Cat, who burst out the door into the carport followed by the rest of Daddy's sisters, all loud and happy. They chirped all at once like a flock of songbirds. The women closed in on Daddy, forming a tight circle, attempting to hug him all at once. One of the older women took Jeff from Mother's arms, cooing over him. Another bent in front of me. "Lord, Glover, she looks just like you."

For a second I filled with pride. I wanted to look like my handsome father.

Daddy smiled. He actually smiled. He was happy to see

his sisters.

The flurry of talking silenced as we entered the kitchen. Then another round of hugs and kisses assaulted us. The house was busting at the seams with people who knew me, but I didn't know them. The scent of turkey and dressing attacked me and my stomach grumbled. On the wall was a black rotary phone with a long, long cord. A real phone. I had seen one at Granny's the night before but wasn't allowed to touch it. In my aunt's large den sat a twenty-five-inch black-and-white TV playing the Macy's Parade live from New York City. I plopped on the floor with my nose almost touching the screen.

"Sit back, Ann," Mother yelled from kitchen.

I moved a half of an inch and marveled at the giant balloons.

"Don't bother her, Jeanette. She's watching the parade. Let her have fun." This was Aunt Cat speaking in her smooth, clear Southern voice. My surroundings dropped away, and I was there with the parade watchers in the crisp, cold New York morning. I'm not sure how long I sat there before the air began to tingle with electric tension. Mother sat at a table in the middle of the large kitchen with pine cabinets. Her high-pitched tone broke through my childhood bliss. The magic vanished, replaced by the rise and fall of women's voices, words dissipating before reaching my ears.

"Ann, do you want to try the phone? Your mom says you've never used one." Aunt Cat stood beside me in her tight-fitting red pants and white blouse. She wore a lot of eye makeup and glossy red lipstick, with fingernails the same color. Her expression told me she thought it odd that I had never used a phone. "Come along with me." She escorted me to her bedroom, where a pink princess phone sat on the table next to the bed. I knew what it was because my Barbie had one. A princess phone.

"I told your father to come help you but he's outside smoking and talking to the boys. You know men." She gave a laugh. "Do you want me to tell you how to use it?"

"Yes ma'am."

"Goodness, you know your manners. Put the receiver to your ear."

The dial tone was loud.

"Who do you want to call?"

Who indeed?

"How about your grandmother?" Aunt Cat suggested.

"Yes."

"Dial her number." She nodded toward the phone.

"I don't know it."

"Wait. I'll find out." She walked to the door and shouted, "Jeanette, what is your mother's phone number?"

Mother answered, and Aunt Cat called out the numbers to me. The phone rang. One, two, three.

"Hello?"

"It's me, Ann. I'm here at Aunt Cat's on the phone," I said in a quiet voice.

Aunt Cat smiled and walked out of the bedroom.

Granny's laugh was light. "Annie, I know who this is. I just can't believe you're finally home."

And for the first time, I began to think all our problems might solve themselves.

When we got back to Granny's, Daddy refused to leave the car. He told Mother to take us in the house. She began to bargain with him, explaining she would do better, that she didn't care what he had done in Germany. That they were making a fresh start. This talk turned into tears, loud, gut-wrenching sobs, then screaming. Jeff joined the chaotic chorus with his cries. Granny came out the front door of her cottage and begged Mother in her quiet, strained but stern voice to come in the house. Mother shoved Daddy, attempting to grab the car keys. She wanted to keep his precious car. "You can't take it. Me and the kids won't have a way to go anywhere." He moved toward her as if he might hit her but didn't. He was leaving us. Leaving me. He knew how Mother felt about me since Jeff's birth. He knew what she was capable of, but he left me anyway. I stood in the yard and watched the taillights of his car disappear. I did not cry. I refused to cry. I stood there as the sun dipped behind the trees and the lights from the neighbor's house lit the yard in patches of golden light.

Granny placed a hand on my shoulder. "Time to come inside. He's not coming back."

She had to be lying. Daddy wouldn't leave me. He would come back. I needed him.

"Come in. I have some cake. You can sleep in my bed tonight."

That's when I broke down. The sobs escaped my chest. She walked me in the house and rocked me while I cried. When Granny felt like enough was enough, she led me to the kitchen and sat me at the table. After a slice of warm pound cake, I went to her four-poster bed and scooted near the window. Granny hummed a silly soft song.

When sleep washed over me, it was the best rest I'd had in months.

Eight Months Later

The white twin sheet stuck to my skinny nine-year-old body as I lay on my back and pushed my head against the screen of the open window at the head of my bed. The steamy Georgia night air sat heavy in the trees. Almost visible. The stars winked in the vast, inky sky. Heat bugs hummed and chirped a song, a beat in my imagination. A magic carpet, on the horizon, out of sight, flew my way so I could escape this house, escape this life. *Go while you can. Leave when the chance comes.*

"Ann, are you asleep?" Mother's voice barged into the magic. Her dark form shifted in the full-size bed beside mine, so close she took a lock of my thin, light-brown hair in her fingers.

A breath, deep and long, threatened to escape when I spoke. "No."

"What are you doing?" The sound of her voice disengaged my dream, my wish.

"Thinking." One-word answers proved easiest in those days.

"You need to go to sleep so I can rest." Her words turned fuzzy.

Her pills would soon enough send her into a deep sleep. "Ok."

"Good. Now, please." Mother's breaths became a rhythm. My thoughts wrapped around and through each one, moving with her, through her, to a place made of dreams. In and out. A slight breeze blew through the branches into the window, kissing my body. I fell into the feathery world of peace.

"I miss your dad." The words, a whisper, a breath leaving

her body, landed in her fingertips, running through my hair, rushing over my scalp, jarring, unwanted.

Daddy. Daddy. Daddy. Maybe I could step through the window into the limbs of the giant oak and climb to the highest point, touch the stars. Maybe. Maybe I was too much of a worrier to escape, to wrestle the long list of why I had to stay put in the room. Our room. Mother and me and Jeff. Crowded together with boxes, many, stacked against the walls. Remnants of our life in Germany, packed away in pasteboard, suffocating us.

When her light snores came in a steady pace, I slid out of the bed, tiptoeing across the creaky sunporch's wooden floor, into Granny's bedroom, and finally, through the door into the living room. I paused, looking back, listening, waiting for Mother to call me.

"It's too hot to sleep, Annie." The opened window above the sofa where Granny reclined didn't help the heat. She never looked away from the new black-and-white twenty-five-inch TV, like the one my aunt had.

I sat in the upholstered swivel rocking chair. Moving back and forth, calm spreading through my chest—the place where worry resided—into my legs and arms. "Yes." In the kitchen window was an air-conditioning unit. Silent. The words, the question—why not turn on the air?—lodged in my throat.

Granny looked over her shoulder at me, reading my mind like she always did. "We don't use the air unless the temperature goes to a hundred. The electric bill will be too high."

She was poor because we lived there now.

"Annie, you're lucky to have a house, this place to live, now that your dad left. Just up and left. I tried to tell Jeanette he would do this. He did the same thing to his first wife. Left her as soon as their son was born. Something about that man doesn't like sons."

But I knew better. I knew it was Mother's crazy ways that put us here. I knew it was Daddy who found another woman. I knew more than Granny could ever know.

"You're lucky to have your mother. Remember that. I know she is different from other mothers and worse now than ever, but times are hard since your dad left. She has to get better. Life will work out." But her voice didn't convince me of this. "I know what it's like to lose a mother. You don't want that. No child ever wants that."

"I know." The thought made my chest hurt.

"Now, go and cut yourself a big piece of that pear cake we cooked this morning. That will make you feel better." She fed Mother like this and complained about the weight Mother put on.

I cut a large piece. I didn't gain weight. The cake was buttery and moist. Tangy with fresh pears soaked in sugar. At least I had my granny. My parents were a mess, but I had her.

"Annie, always look out for your family. They are all you have in this life. Don't turn your back on them. Don't take them for granted. You will always love your mama no matter what." Her words were wispy, and because we could read each other's minds, I knew she was thinking of her own mother.

"Tell me about your mama," I said around my next big bite.

"I only remember her quiet smile. And her love. Always her love."

And as she told me the story again, probably for the tenth time since we arrived in her house months earlier, the invisible pouch around my neck weighed more, another stone added.

Part Two:

Asalee Malinda Redd Hawkins

Stone 2
A Harsh Legacy

In August 1915 Asalee Redd Hawkins, a thirty-eight-year-old mother of nine, died in the Hightower Community of Forsyth County, Georgia. With Asalee's death, an obscure legacy that mattered only to my family was born. This story was at the core of all the legends told among the Hawkins family. Asalee's death became the tale of time and place, of ignorance and casualties, of living in the Deep South in a part of history where people took the law in their own hands to make justice fit their ideals. This story is the map back through the years that marked the path of choices made by Henry Lee Hawkins, Asalee's husband. One known photo of Asalee and Henry Lee exists. Asalee is seated next to Henry Lee. Her two oldest children, both boys, stand beside her. On her lap is the couple's baby daughter, who looks large in Asalee's delicately petite arms. Asalee's face is stolid. There is no indication that she struggled to be what her husband expected or to prove wrong her parents' foreboding about her chosen union. She sat for the portrait. She wanted to preserve her small, beautiful family. Always the good wife and mother. Her duty fulfilled.

After the family photo was taken in 1904, Henry Lee and Asalee went on to have nine more children. Inas Elene Hawkins, my granny, was their seventh child and six years old when her mama died. Her memories were vivid, detailed. Children in 1915 were more mature than kids raised in future generations. People in the rural foothills of the North Georgia Mountains, the gateway to Appalachia, lived in a sideways world, filled with problems, that wouldn't follow a set of rules society had written. Parents, try as they might, couldn't shield children from ugliness. Inas spent much of her life attempting to forget the last day she spent with Asalee.

Inas and her father Henry Lee, her mother Asalee, and her six-month-old baby sister Mary set out for a day trip to town, probably Atlanta. The purpose for the adventure was to buy Inas some new Sunday shoes for church.

Her family, like most families at the time, faithfully attended church. Friendship Baptist Church was co-founded in 1840 by F. M. Hawkins, Henry Lee's great-great-uncle. On September 5, 1840, the church body, eleven members, voted that F. M. Hawkins become their first preacher. The minutes showed that the first meeting addressed the need of a building. The group agreed on dimensions and to building the structure with logs.

As Inas left home that hot August day in 1915, she couldn't believe her luck. The older brothers and sisters were left behind to do chores. She claimed her place in the back of the family Model T Ford in a rumble seat. Henry Lee drove, and Asalee held baby Mary on her lap. Inas sat tall and proud, waving as they passed the other farms, sticking her tongue out at one girl who always made fun of her in church. Nothing could dampen the thrill of going to town. As Hightower fell behind them and the empty road stretched in front, Inas imagined she was on her way to a different world, maybe somewhere like Hollywood where they made the silent films that Beatrice, her older sister, loved so much. She was so deep in thought she didn't notice Henry Lee begin to scream at Asalee. Inas had a tolerance for his anger, so a few minutes went by before her worry surfaced and gnawed at her stomach. Henry Lee's face turned red, along with his ears—a sure sign he was more than angry. His words disappeared into the wind, dissolving before reaching Inas. But the way Henry Lee jabbed the air with one hand suggested his mood had escalated into a place where Inas needed to beware. The churning of the engine turned quiet, silent. A swift movement, a shadow, a blur, passed in front of her. The world slowed, twirled, froze. Asalee slumped sideways and her seat was empty. No Mary or Mama. Gone. The Model T ground gears as it came to a stop. Henry Lee jumped from the seat and walked behind the Model T. Inas turned to look, slow, neck creaking like the rusty hinges of the kitchen garden gate. Try as she did, she couldn't form the image, the memory, of Asalee on the ground or in the road. Or Mary crying. Surely she was. What Inas saw next was Asalee sitting in the front seat again with Mary on her lap. Her beautiful wide-brim riding hat was gone. The quiet was the darkest of sounds. Henry Lee put the Model T in gear and lurched forward with a jerk as Asalee's shoulders shook with silent sobs.

Later when Inas was grown, she would tell family members a watered-down version of what happened that day. What child wouldn't make the scene more manageable? Asalee was getting out of the Model T at the store, Inas said, and her buttoned-up boot heel caught the running board and pitched her backwards. She whacked her head good on the curb. Inas told this story so often that she believed it as the truth, but in her dreams she saw Asalee's face, her tears, the missing hat caught in the wind, twirling away.

Henry Lee drove to the store, and the whole family went

in and bought shoes, brand new black patent leather, shiny like the sun hanging in the hazy blue sky that day. The car ride home was uneventful. Inas began to wonder if the incident ever happened. Maybe she had fallen asleep and dreamed the whole scene.

The next morning, Henry Lee, Inas's oldest brother Elbert, and Ernest, the next to oldest, went to the cotton fields with the paid laborers at dawn. Beatrice, age thirteen, took charge of looking after the little ones with some help from eight-year-old Bertha. Their mother Asalee went back to bed because she felt dizzy, sick to her stomach, just not herself at all. Her words sounded funny, slurred like when Henry Lee had too much shine to drink. Never in all of Inas's memories was there a time when Asalee went back to bed during the day except when Stella Mae and Mary were born. Inas worried another baby was coming, and that was the last thing she wanted. The more babies, the more Inas would have to watch in a couple of years when she was old enough. And as much as she hated Beatrice and her bossy ways, she understood a girl didn't want to be a mama to her younger brothers and sisters.

Before the afternoon meal was placed on the table, Bertha went to check on Asalee and returned to get Beatrice. Then the two of them came out of Asalee's room, issuing orders for Inas to stay put with the younger kids. Bertha and Beatrice ran out of the house. What was Inas supposed to do with a baby and toddler? She was only six. Later, after everything was said and done, Bertha told Inas what she found when she checked on Asalee: her whole head was black and she didn't know her daughters.

When Inas was a grown woman, her doctor explained that Asalee must have had a brain bleed caused from the blow to her head when pushed from the moving car. An accident victim could seem normal after this kind of trauma. He called it "talk and die" syndrome. Some people could remain normal for a few days; most, like Asalee, showed deteriorating symptoms in a few hours.

Beatrice and Bertha brought Henry Lee in from the fields. He promptly sent one of the brothers, probably Ernest, for the doctor, who arrived in due time. There was the matter of tracking the man down and making the trip back to the farm. When the doctor did arrive, he examined Asalee all of two minutes, declaring that never before in his "doctoring" career had he seen someone's head turn black. Asalee was William Poole and Sarah Redd's oldest child, their firstborn. The Redds were a well-respected family in the community. The doctor urged that Asalee be taken to the hospital in Atlanta. But she never left the house that day. The decision proved fatal, though in fairness she wouldn't have lived anyway. Inas went to bed that night without her mother's kiss.

The next morning produced stifling air, squeezing through the open bedroom window. The house was silent as Inas crept downstairs. An unspoken feeling swirled through the rooms, off balance but familiar, similar to when she put her shoes on the wrong feet and wore them until someone—probably bossy Beatrice—pointed out her mistake. The sun streaked across the front hall with the light of August heat. She had slept too late. That was it. Asalee would not be happy. In the front room, several people wearing church clothes sat or stood, among them the preacher and his wife. Mama would just throw a fit because Inas was dressed in playclothes. The yard was full of wagons, and even Grandpa Redd's automobile was parked to the side of the house. Everyone around the county knew the Redds, and there were a lot of them, mostly doing better than the rest of their neighbors. Inas had heard Henry Lee say this over and over as if it were a curse. But she knew it was these grandparents, her mama's parents, that gave her family the wonderful Model T. She liked being a Redd, was proud Mama was one. Talk among the adults had Henry Lee at a disadvantage in his marriage. Even though the Hawkins family were co-founders of the Friendship Baptist Church, Henry's branch hadn't stayed put. Her grandmother and grandfather on the Hawkins side had moved far away so they could own their farm. Asalee brought more to their marriage than Henry Lee.

Inas's stomach grumbled, but she didn't dare go to the kitchen. Mama would surely feel better and be running the preparation of the afternoon meal. She would have Inas's hide for sleeping so late and forgetting whatever special day she had forgotten. Asalee had only been mad at Inas once. Like most little girls, she worried about pleasing her parents, but in Inas's case it was Asalee's approval she sought on most occasions, seeing how Henry Lee didn't give the small kids a lot of attention and the older ones didn't want him to notice. Normally Asalee spoke in a quiet, even voice, but the week before when she caught Inas in the hog pen, she had screamed at the top of her lungs and nearly jerked Inas's arm out of its socket, pulling her over the fence. Little girls could be killed by large hogs. All Inas had wanted was a good look at the new litter of piglets, pink and full of squeals.

So something had to be done to make Asalee happy with Inas on this morning with all the surprise guests. She decided to please her mama by dressing in her Sunday best like all the other visitors, and she would do this alone with no help from her older sisters. Of course this gave her the perfect excuse to wear her new Sunday shoes, purchased the day before.

Dressed and polished to her best ability, Inas began the descent down the stairs. Daddy's voice filled the room below. He was as loud as Mama was quiet. And that morning he sounded angrier than ever. Inas made a snap decision to slide out the front door instead.

The creek on the edge of the pasture ran fast from the rain that fell during the night. This didn't stop Inas from jumping on the old log that Clyde, another older brother, had wedged between the banks two days before. He had dared her to cross, and she had done so without a problem. Bertha fell with the first try, and she was older by two years. Clyde had warned that neither of them should come there alone, or he would beat the tar out of them. He loved to act like he was their father. That was because he had Daddy's name as his middle name, Clyde Henry Hawkins. Inas rarely liked Clyde—he was pure mean especially to animals—but he was her brother and the good book said she had to love all her brothers and sisters.

Inas loved Elbert the best because he was kind and quiet like Asalee. This similarity caused Elbert a lot of problems with Henry Lee, who wanted his oldest son to be more like him. To be a man. Elbert was the recipient of Henry Lee's wrath on most days. And if not for Asalee, Elbert might not have survived some of the beatings.

Three steps across the log and all was fine, proving Clyde was just a big fat worrywart. With the fourth step, Inas's foot slipped. The murky deep water jumped toward her. She plunged in head first. When she stood, her new shoes sank deep into the miry mud, making her toes squishy. A spanking would be in order, and hopefully Daddy wouldn't be the one to deliver the blows. Wails that resembled a dying animal erupted from deep down in her chest as she climbed the muddy bank, smearing her dress with the red Georgia clay.

Elbert found her in the pasture. Her heart cracked open with the thought of him being disappointed in her. His face was stern, and old man lines marked his forehead. He looked at her as if a muddy girl in her best Sunday clothes was the most normal thing on that farm. His lips tightened. "Mama passed during the night, Inas."

"Passed where?"

He sighed. "Mama died from hitting her head."

There it was. The worst news a child could hear. The stuff of nightmares. The stupid black shoes didn't matter. There would be no spanking. Inas wished she could trade a beating from Daddy just to have her mama. Not one person in the house had shaken Inas awake to tell her that her mama had passed on to Heaven. Dead. That couldn't be right. Mothers didn't die. But the whole story was true. Mama was dead. Inas was motherless.

Asalee was buried near the church in a plot that looked out on the mountain in the distance. She was buried that very day with no time to get to used to the idea, as if Inas ever could. Her wedding ring quilt was placed inside the pine box made early that morning by Elbert and Ernest, and now her body lay inside the casket in a wagon drawn by two of Grandpa Redd's best horses. Folks followed the wagon in their own, or walked slowly, as if they too dreaded the job ahead. Inas walked beside Beatrice. She tried not to think about getting a drink of water. Instead, she worried over what would happen to her now that Asalee was dead.

Later, a big, beautiful marble stone, taller than Inas, was erected at the head of her mama's grave. On it was written, *She died as she lived, a Christian.* But it was the words *wife of Henry Lee* that sent a shiver up Inas's spine each time she read them. Would Asalee have liked that claim after all she had been through? Seeing how it was Henry Lee who pushed her from the moving automobile? As a child Inas would visit the cemetery only a few times, but always she remembered the regal stone that marked this great woman's resting place.

But that's not where the story ends. Does a mother's dying ever end? There is a new life to acclimate oneself to. And in the confusion of this adjustment, a six-year-old might see things different, or tell herself a story she could live with rather than the truth. Maybe this event would begin a trend in storytelling, adjusting the facts.

As a grown woman, Inas would tell this story: twelve days after Asalee's death, August 17, 1915, Inas stood in her front yard. The sun moved through the stand of pines. She kicked at rocks. A commotion came roaring down the road that ran in front of the family home. Dust hung at top of the trees, and voices rang in the air, mixed with a loud rattling sound. Several Model Ts—men yelling, some waving guns—came toward her.

"Those men had the Jew, Leo Frank, who killed Mary Phagan at the pencil factory. He was already dead, bleeding from a wound to his throat. The blood was all down his long white shirt."

The story Granny told me never changed or grew like some of her other tales. I was nine the first time she recited this story, and she continued telling it until she died in 1993 at the age of eighty-three. My heart broke fresh with every telling. But her story was wrong. The pieces don't fit with historical fact. Inas did tell part of the truth: in all likelihood the truth of the story was the convoy with Leo Frank as she claimed. But she changed the place where she witnessed the sight of Leo Frank, and another key fact of this story was wrong. Who could blame her for changing things? Or maybe that is how her young mind protected her from the reality of what really took place.

The events leading up to the morning of August 17th ensured the lynching of Leo Frank. During the afternoon of the 16th, a group of twenty-five men from Marietta, Georgia—some forty miles southwest of Hightower—boarded seven cars and made their way through the Georgia countryside, southbound with one purpose in mind. They wanted to take the law into their own hands since Governor John Slaton had commuted Leo Frank's sentence of death to life in prison. Many of the twenty-five men were part of the Marietta and Cobb County judicial system and felt they had to right the injustice made toward the Phagan family. In their minds, the actions they took were spurred by civic duty. So were the claims. Around nine that night, they reached the outskirts of the state prison farm in Milledgeville, where they cut the phone wires to the town so help could not be called. They took Leo Frank, wearing only his white monogrammed nightshirt, from his protective cell where he had been placed to recover from a throat wound inflicted by a fellow prisoner. He was due to go back into the prison population only days after he was taken by the quiet mob.

The group of vigilantes took to the road again but lost one of the cars in the convoy to mechanical problems. In the early morning hours, just before dawn, between 5:30 and 7:00 am of August 17th, the cars passed Henry Lee's farm. In all likelihood, Henry Lee placed his family in his Model T and followed the mob from a distance, as many others did that day. Because as secret as the men wanted to be in Milledgeville, they didn't bother the closer they came to their destination. The group had made their travels into the foothills of North Georgia to confuse those who might attempt to stop them, and one has to ask if they wanted to show off their captive to the many supporters in the surrounding area. What must be remembered is that most people agreed with the death penalty Leo Frank received.

Inas must have wondered why she was being taken from her home at daybreak on a car ride. Maybe she was frightened. Maybe she already knew from Henry Lee speaking of the men's intentions. This wouldn't have been the first time she was faced with exposure to an angry mob, and she knew her father was capable of violence.

As the sun rode the treetops, the convoy barreled through Roswell and took Roswell Road, crossing the long covered bridge* over the Chattahoochee River. The mob's intention that day had been to lynch Leo Frank over the grave of Mary Phagan, but word leaked to the newspapers, and reporters were waiting there. The mob did not want to be identified in the papers, so they stopped at Frey's Gin,† a few miles from Mary's

* By 1930 this bridge would be replaced with a stronger one.

† There were twenty-six lynchers involved with Leo Frank's hanging. William J. Frey was the former sheriff of Cobb County from 1903–1909. He owned the land where Frank was hanged and prepared the noose used to lynch him. Stories have him placing the noose around Frank's neck him-

grave, where there was a wooded area and a sturdy table. Mr. Frank would need a surface where he could stand while the noose was placed around his neck and his sentence was enforced. When the table was knocked out from underneath Mr. Frank's bound feet, his head snapped and his struggle was so ferocious that he ripped open the throat wound. Blood ran down the front of his white nightshirt. Leo Frank was not hurt while the men transported him to his lynching. The only way Inas could have seen Mr. Frank bleeding and already dead was by attending the aftermath of the lynching. Over a thousand people were at Frey's Gin to sightsee by 8:30 that morning. Inas was one of them.

She would always remember Asalee's death in unison with Leo Frank's lynching. The two events were blended into one. In 1983 I was visiting Granny at her home in Dunwoody, Georgia. A news story came on the TV. Eighty-five-year-old Alonzo Mann, former office boy for Leo Frank, admitted that he had seen Jim Conely, the murderer of Mary Phagan, carrying her limp body in the pencil factory that fateful April afternoon in 1913 while the Confederate Memorial Parade took place. Conely threatened Alonzo with death if he breathed a word. Alonzo's mother told her son to keep quiet because they didn't need to get involved. She believed Frank would never be convicted because he was innocent. Justice would prevail. But that's not what happened.

This news story shocked Granny. She, like so many who came to view Leo Frank's body that day, believed this man had

---

self. See Donald E. Wilkes Jr., "Steve Oney's List of the Leo Frank Lynchers," May 5, 2004, *flagpole*, https://flagpole.com/news/news-features/2004/05/05/steve-oney-s-list-of-the-leo-frank-lynchers.

committed the murder. How could she believe otherwise? If she did, that would make her father and all the adults in the woods of Frey's Gin morally responsible in some way for the lynching of an innocent man. That was a bitter reality to chew.

"I'll never forget seeing the way that poor man looked that day," she said, speaking of Frank. "No man, no matter what he did, deserved to die in such a way." She looked toward the television, at the face of Alonzo Mann. "But now this old man is telling things he should keep to himself, clearing his conscience. That's just plain foolish, nothing but trouble. Everyone knows the Jew killed the Phagan girl. Some things are better just left buried and not thought about anymore. He needs to be quiet, take it to his grave. He won't help anyone now."

And these words from Granny told me she knew exactly how Asalee had died. She knew Henry Lee did indeed push his wife from a moving car. She had witnessed it. His actions were not something she dreamed. Inas watched her mother receive the injury that would kill her just as she witnessed Leo Frank's lifeless body hanging from the oak tree. Pain and shame had turned both of these events into her dark secrets.

Isn't that where most of our problems begin? Isn't it shame that keeps us from speaking truths, our truths? The story of Henry Lee killing his wife, Asalee, was the family legacy of shame. This story was the backbone of Granny's history, my family history. It would haunt us throughout generations, as if Asalee was a haint standing in a shadowy corner.

Stone 3
Untold Stories

Every family has a foundation, shaky or solid, most of the time a little of both. The Redds, Asalee's side of the family, had roots that ran deep in Barnwell and Orangeburg, South Carolina. Job Redd Sr., Asalee's third great-grandfather, shows up in this area in the early 1700s. In his will from 1809 there is a list of property: a horse, a saddle, a cow hide, thirteen head of hogs, and two sows, among other items. In the 1790 census the household of Asalee's great-great-grandfather, Job Redd Jr., consisted of two males over sixteen and four females. One of the four females was Edi Bently Redd, his wife. Job Jr. was born in 1753 and died November 24, 1839. He was a Revolutionary War soldier.*

The couple's son, James Redd, was born in 1785. This was Asalee's great-grandfather. James married Martha Boyet in 1809 in South Carolina when Martha was eighteen and James was twenty-four. In 1828, Job Redd Jr. was part of the Cherokee land lottery because he was wounded in the Revolutionary War. The whole family moved to the land Job was awarded, including his son James and daughter-in-law Martha. Their son Thomas Lafayette Redd, Job Jr.'s grandson, was born in Forsyth County around where Friendship Baptist Church

---

* Job Redd Jr. is listed in the South Carolina Patriot Roster. He is listed as John Redd married to Edi Bently with the notation, "He was wounded by the Tories." (Boby Gilmer Moss, *Roster of South Carolina Patriots in the American Revolution* [Baltimore, MD: Genealogical Publishing Co., 1994])

would be built in 1840.

Inas was blessed with examples of strong women. Malinda, her paternal great-grandmother, was one of them. Though Inas would never meet her, Malinda would leave her with several examples of determination and strength that must have encouraged Inas to stand tall and be tough. I can imagine Asalee telling her daughters, including Inas, stories about her grandmother.

Thomas and Malinda married in May 1846, probably in Friendship Baptist Church, where Thomas's family were members. The couple began their family soon after. At the age of thirty-five, Thomas went off to fight in the Civil War with the Cherokee Legion, also known as the Georgia State Guards, as a private. Thomas first fought in Kentucky, then moved out to Mississippi and East Louisiana. Malinda was left at home with seven children, ranging from age thirteen to a newborn. Thomas endured the hardships of the battle of Vicksburg, and the Cherokee Legion was captured on July 4, 1863. After this battle he managed to be part of Palmer's and Johnston's Battalion of Artillery instead of a prisoner of war. He found himself fighting in the Tennessee campaigns.

While Thomas was away, the couple's eight-year-old daughter, Martha, died. Malinda walked through this grief without her husband. Communications in the battlefield were less than optimal. It is quite possible that Thomas came home from war—years after the event—to learn for the first time that his daughter had died. Inas's grandfather, William Poole Redd, was five years old when the war began and nine when it ended. So the two had to get to know each other all over again when Thomas came home. Two years later, in 1867, Malinda gave birth to twins, a boy and a girl, bringing the total to nine children. Maybe this was the couple's way of beginning again, holding on to what was precious in their life. They were somehow able to keep their farm, which wasn't the case for many.

In March 1877, two months before Inas's mother, Asalee, was born, Malinda died. Thomas and Malinda's son William Poole would name his first child after his mother, leaving Asalee large shoes to fill. Malinda was fifty-four when she died and still had nine-year-old twins who depended on her.

By 1880, Thomas remarried twenty-nine-year-old Lucy Terry, who had been raised in Hightower near Friendship Baptist Church and brought along Martha, her daughter from a previous marriage. The new couple would go on to have two sons, Martin Luther and Stephen Clyde, and a daughter, Zemma. By this time, Thomas was sixty years old, and by all accounts the couple had a good union. Thomas died at age sixty-six in 1893. Sixteen-year-old Asalee attended her grandfather's funeral and sat near her step-grandmother, Lucy, and her children. Thomas was buried in Friendship Baptist Church Cemetery—not far from where Asalee would be buried twenty-two years later—next to Malinda, so strong was his love for his first wife. Lucy went on to live until 1944 and witnessed three major wars: Civil War, World War I, and World War II. She died at the age of ninety-four and was buried in the infamous Westview Cemetery in Atlanta. She never remarried.

Because of the time in history, Asalee probably struggled to view herself as a strong woman, but she was surrounded by stories of women with substance, women who left a mark on her life. As her mother, Sarah Tollison Redd, said, she came from good stock. Sarah was a woman who outlived her daughter and husband, dying at the age of eighty-two in 1937.

Henry Lee Hawkins, too, had a powerful family with heavy male influences. Henry Lee was born on December 25, 1875, to Claiborn and Georgia Hawkins. His family can be traced back to William Hawkins and Sarah Foster, both born in 1785. Two of their sons were of significance to Henry Lee. Fredrick Marshall (F. M.) Hawkins, his great-great-uncle, moved to Georgia from South Carolina and helped found Friendship Baptist Church in 1840. Baylis E. Hawkins, F. M.'s younger brother and Henry Lee's great-great-grandfather, followed him. Baylis married Jane Hawkins. They had many children, and their third, John Lee, born in 1834, would be Henry Lee's grandfather.

John Lee Hawkins married Nancy E. Lewis from Charleston, South Carolina, on January 29, 1854. John Lee would go off to fight the Civil War at the age of twenty-seven in 1861. He would be captured on May 14, 1864, fighting at the Battle of Resaca,[†] and taken to Alton, Illinois,[‡] as a prisoner of war.

[†] "Fought on May 14–15, 1864, the Battle of Resaca was the first major engagement of the Atlanta campaign in the Civil War (1861–1865). Situated on the north bank of the Oostanaula River approximately seventy-five miles northwest of Atlanta, Resaca was located on the strategically important Western and Atlantic Railroad. The fighting at Resaca demonstrated that the outnumbered Confederate Army could only slow but not stop the advance of Union forces into Georgia" (Kevin W. Young, "Battle of Resaca," June 18, 2010, *New Georgia Encyclopedia*, https://www.georgiaencyclopedia.org/articles/history-archaeology/battle-resaca).

[‡] The Alton prison opened in 1833 as a state penitentiary and closed in 1860. The prison became a Military Prison in early 1862 when members of the 13th US Infantry were assigned as guards. Throughout the war, 11,764 Confederate prisoners passed through the gates. Not only soldiers were kept there. Several women were imprisoned there for treasonable actions by making anti-Union statements, aiding and escaped Confederate, etc. Conditions in the prison were horrible and the death rate was high. Up

This record has him listed as part of the 56th regiment in Georgia. He wasn't released until June 15, 1865. John Lee walked home—a two- to three-month journey—like many prisoners and soldiers at that time.

John Lee and Nancy would have five children. Their first was Claiborn Augustus, who would become Henry Lee's father. John Lee showed up in the 1880 census living in Crossroads, close to what is now Woodstock, Georgia, and gravely sick with consumption. He died shortly after the census taker came to his house. He was forty-six.

Henry Lee grew up with Asalee at Friendship Baptist Church. He had a reputation for being a flirt, and Sarah must have warned her daughter against any interest in him. In the Hawkins's household, Georgia Ann would have warned her firstborn son that the Redds provided Asalee with a life he could never measure up to. Despite the warnings, the couple married on Sunday, January 12, 1896, in front of the congregation at Friendship Baptist Church right after the morning service. He was twenty-two and she was nineteen. Henry Lee was handsome enough, sporting a handlebar mustache. Asalee was petite and quiet but pretty in a natural way, with high cheekbones and dark hair pulled back from her angular face.

The young newlyweds moved into their own home on the same road as Henry Lee's parents, Claiborn and Georgia. Henry Lee rented his farm from someone else. This meant he was a sharecropper, paying a portion of money from his crops to the landlord. On August 15, 1897, Asalee gave birth to their

---

to three-hundred prisoners and soldiers died and are buried on the island now under water. ("Alton Prison," *Alton in the Civil* War, available at http://www.altonweb.com/history/civilwar/confed/)

first child, a boy named Elbert Linton Hawkins. Next came Ernest Floyd Hawkins on April 7, 1900. Asalee wouldn't live to hear the stories about Ernest becoming a force to be reckoned with and how he would turn out to be the son who saved the family from Henry Lee's choices. All this would be years in the future. As she held this second son in her arms, little Elbert looking on, she only wished that her sons would grow to be strong, good men. She wanted Elbert and Ernest to get along, hoping they would be like any brothers with three years difference between them, playing and fighting, protecting each other at all costs from others outside the family. Asalee and Henry Lee would go on to have two more sons, but Elbert and Ernest were the most treasured, Asalee having a soft spot for Elbert and Henry Lee choosing Ernest. As both boys grew into manhood, Ernest acted more like the oldest sibling, taking many adult responsibilities.

On May 19, 1902, Asalee gave birth to her first daughter, Bessie Beatrice Hawkins, completing the family as they appear in the only existing photograph of them. Asalee is twenty-six in the picture, a fully mature woman for that time in history. Little does she know that in twelve years she will die by the hand of her husband. There is a trace of Inas in her stare, but mostly resolve, maybe even surrender, as if she had accepted that her life was as good as things would get. But many women in the early 1900s were photographed with the same expressions. It was a trying time to be a woman, especially in the rural South. Once a woman married a man, she had no rights unless he granted them. Women had to be very careful with their choices in matrimony. If the isolation of the rural area was mixed with family expectations and young men "up for picking"—as Inas would say—it was easy to see why some couples were so ill-fitted for each other. Most women—including Asalee and generations before her—learned the art of settling, how to adjust their dreams with reality. This hardened some women, making them bitter, while other women focused on being good mothers to their children and attempted to look beyond their husbands' flaws. Asalee was the latter.

Clyde Henry Hawkins, the third son, was born on February 10, 1904. He was named after his father, a legacy he would fulfill in many ways.

By the time Inas was born on June 22, 1909, there were six brothers and sisters ahead of her. One brother, Glinn, was born on April 1, 1906, and he died just over a year later on June 21, 1907. Tragedy had struck the family in the worst way. Asalee was a grieving mother and still trying look after another newborn, Bertha Georgia, born on April 3, 1907. Infant deaths were more numerous in the early 1900s, especially in the foothills and mountains of Appalachia, but the recorded statistic becomes something larger and more meaningful when one has a face to go with the numbers. Little Glinn's death right after Bertha was born was the first story told about Asalee. Her solemn face in that old photograph seems to reflect that she knew exactly what she had taken on by marrying Henry Lee and how much grief she would live through in her short lifetime.

Inas's birth came in that time of year when the last of spring gives up and the heat and humidity of summer presses down on the mountains and valleys. Asalee and Henry Lee were an old married couple in more ways than one. Rumors in the small rural community flew like a flash fire through dry brush. Asalee chose to take the high road and ignore what her neighbors whispered about Henry Lee behind her back: that her husband had someone on the side who was seventeen years his junior. This was no fly-by-night affair. The two of them had been seen throughout the local communities on more than one occasion. Asalee found it easier to pretend ignorance. Henry Lee was known for his temper and love of moonshine, and she wouldn't want to bring out his anger by confronting him. Folks enjoyed gossiping about those who had more money and more material things. Asalee's family didn't hurt for anything. In a time when many others struggled to get in their cotton, Henry Lee was able to hire help. This was in large part due to his in-laws. Asalee's father William was no stranger to success. In 1870 when he was thirteen, his father, Thomas, owned a farm worth $640.00—a small fortune in the four years after the Civil War—and his personal assets amounted to $540.00. William must have wanted the best for his only daughter and oldest child. While Henry Lee lived in Hightower, he never owned his farm. The Redds had learned to live with their son in-law, but they heard the rumors of infidelity and drunkenness. And they knew the other shoe would fall.

Inas arrived not only into a turbulent home but also into an area that wasn't a peaceful place. The small communities of Oscarville, Big Creek, and Settlendown had their share of turmoil. In fall 1912, when Inas was almost three and a half, two white women were raped—Ellen Grice and Mae Crow. Ms. Crow died from her injuries two weeks after the attack. Two African American teenage boys, Ernest Knox and Oscar Daniels, were arrested and taken to Atlanta for safekeeping for the kidnapping, rape, and beating of Mae Crow. Murder charges were added once she died. Rob Edwards, also African American, was arrested too, but a mob of over a thousand men rushed the jail in Cumming and took him, beating him to death with crowbars. Then Edwards was tied to the back of a truck with a chain and dragged around the square of Cumming. Despite Inas's young age, she remembered clearly Rob Edwards's beaten face—and described it in her stories more than one time—as his body was pulled near her family where they stood in the town. Henry Lee had wanted his family to see justice visited upon Mr. Edwards. He was probably part of the mob.

"One of the worst sights I have ever seen was that poor man strung up on the light pole in the square," Inas always said as she closed this story.

When it came time for the trial of Ernest Knox and Oscar Daniels, Henry Lee was chosen to serve on Daniels's jury. The jury selection and trial for both boys took place in a matter of a day, running deep into the night. Both young men were found guilty and sentenced to death by hanging for the beating and rape and eventual death of Mae Crow. Without any evidence that placed Knox and Daniels at the crime scene, Henry Lee, along with the entire jury, found the boys guilty and sentenced them to death.

The October hanging day had the atmosphere of a country fair as many locals showed up to the execution that the law of Georgia said had to be private. Twenty-four hours before the hanging, the fence erected to provide privacy for the execution was burned to the ground. Inas did not attend this event, but her father Henry Lee was surely there. It seems to fit with his character. Asalee must have tapped into some of the strength passed on to her from the strong women in her family and refused to attend, keeping the younger children with her.

The racial cleansing of African Americans from Forsyth County began the night Mae Crow died a few weeks before Knox and Daniels's trial. From that point on, all able-bodied men were expected to meet at the crossroads of the communities to deliver their nightly raids of justice—in the present, this would be considered domestic terrorism. These men, among them my great-grandfather Henry Lee, had one purpose in mind: destroy the lives of over a thousand people.

The removal of 1,100 African Americans was achieved by breaking windows, shooting at houses, killing animals, and burning down homes. Five African American churches were burned to the ground, and only a visit to Cumming's courthouse can give a person an idea of where these churches stood. Someone driving through the area now will not see many signs of these 1912 communities. There are a few tiered fields that must have been worked by the residents. In places, there are old houses falling in on themselves in the middle of farmland that existed at the time. Mostly there is new growth, large wealthy subdivisions, strip malls, banks, and fast-food restaurants. In 1912, African American families held a mass exodus, leaving with what they could carry; often the land was up for the taking, or these terrified people sold their acres for much less than they were worth. Forsyth County remained white only until 1987, when a demonstration[§] that drew national attention took place and planted the seed of change.

[§] In 1987, Rev. Hosea Williams led a racially mixed group of 75–90 protestors to the courthouse in Cumming, Georgia, situated in Forsyth County. The marchers carried signs. One said, "Give Brotherhood a Chance." A small group of racists also carried signs. One said, "Sickle-Cell Anemia—The Great White Hope." But the real problem began shortly after the marchers turned the corner on Highway 9, where 400–500 mostly male segregationists stood. The protestors believed they were safe because of the uniformed police presence. Racial taunts quickly turned into violence, however, as militant segregationists broke through police lines. The scene was reminiscent of Bloody Sunday in Selma, Alabama, in 1965, some

As an artist with interracial grandchildren, I found this part of my family history particularly sickening—so much so that my shame nearly defeated my writing about Henry Lee. How easy it would have been to gloss over him. But in the end, I swallowed the bitter pill of embarrassment and shame, and remembered this book was written in part to tell Asalee's story. I also wanted to reveal the reasons Inas made the choices she made. Henry Lee was a large part of Asalee and Inas's existences. And the story of how he cut Asalee's life short and left his children motherless needs to be acknowledged.

At home, Inas witnessed a raging father who beat his wife and his sons, especially Elbert, whenever the notion struck him. The day Asalee was buried, Elbert left home never to return. Somehow he made it to Ohio, where he married Mable Ruth Menger. They had two daughters, Alice Ruth and Mary Margaret. His daughter Alice would find Inas years after her father's death, when both women were older. Alice's stories would help Inas understand what kind of life Elbert lived. He had escaped the destiny Inas lived through back in Hightower. She would always be proud that Elbert became a successful and kind man despite his origins. It must have given her permission to forgive her own bad choices. But did she? I never saw an indication that she did.

---

eighteen years earlier. Hosea Williams, activist and member of Martin Luther King Jr.'s inner circle, was struck in the head by a rock. The police were able to regain control, arresting 55 marchers, including David Duke, grand wizard of the Ku Klux Klan, antisemitic conspiracy theorist, and Holocaust denier. See "Forsyth County Civil Rights March, January, 1987," *About North Georgia*, http://www.aboutnorthgeorgia.com/ang/Civil_Rights_March,_January,_1987.

Stone 4
The Fire

Inas read any book she could get her hands on before she started attending school the fall after Asalee died. She had no memories of who taught her to be such an avid reader. Sometimes she would joke, saying she taught herself by stealing her mother's books and staring at the words. Asalee loved to read, and if not for her father bringing her books, she would have been deprived. Books—besides the Bible or the occasional religious text—weren't shelved in the homes of Hightower Community.* Children barely went to school due to their required help on the farms. William Poole Redd, Asalee's father, was an educated man who bought books when he visited Atlanta. And when she became a mother, Asalee insisted that all of her children attend school.

The one-room schoolhouse Inas and her siblings attended contained long benches, like pews in a church, and a potbelly stove in the center, but it had very few of the needed school supplies. Attendance was best in the cold of winter after the crops were harvested. All the grades fit in the one room. A long blackboard stretched down one wall, providing the teacher with a place to write math problems and reading lessons. The teacher was only a little older than twelve-year-old Beatrice. On a good day, each student had a slate tablet to show their work.

---

* The foothills of Appalachia were part of a secluded rural area in the early 1900s. This was before Lake Lanier was built, many farms flooded, and people from the city began moving northeast.

There were primers—books for reading—for the younger students but not enough for the whole school, so sharing was mandated. Inas hated the primers and said they were dull as the paint peeling off a house. The teacher understood she had a smart girl on her hands, even though at the time girls were not encouraged to be smart or to get a lot of "book-learning."

After Asalee died, Ernest and Clyde didn't go back to school. Ernest found a job to help out. He was a resourceful young man who always did what needed to be done to keep life decent for his family. As an adult, he built a Delco system to provide electricity for his home.[†] Clyde stopped going to school because the one person who cared that he received an education was dead. Beatrice left school to fill Asalee's shoes and watch the little ones, Inas included. Inas gladly attended school. She remained an avid student and reader until arthritis made her hands weak in her old age. Then she used a book holder. Finally, her eyesight grew so bad she couldn't see the print no matter how large. The loss of the ability to learn and read in her late seventies/early eighties was like losing her best friends. She never quite recovered.

William Poole Redd and his wife Sarah, Asalee's grieving parents, suffered through the rumors about the circumstances of their daughter's death that season. Hightower and the surrounding communities buzzed with gossip. A code of silence kept neighbors and family members from going to the local

---

[†] Charles F. Kettering introduced the Delco-Light system in 1916. While cities had lights and running water, rural areas didn't. This system helped bring progress to the foothills of Appalachia. See Sam Moore, "The Delco-Light Plant," January 2013, *Farm Collector*, https://www.farmcollector.com/farm-shows/delco-light-plant-zmlz13janzbea.

sheriff in Cumming. Henry Lee was never arrested or questioned for murdering his wife. There is no mention of Asalee's death in records or the newspaper. But this didn't mean Henry Lee went unpunished for his crime. Life in Hightower turned hardscrabble for the family and afforded no time to mourn. Luxuries once given were retracted by the community as a whole and by the Redds specifically. Henry's status in Hightower and surrounding areas was dismissed overnight. The kids were the unfortunate victims of the fallout from these social attacks.

On the first day of school, Inas wore a store-bought dress purchased by Asalee from a department store in Atlanta just for the occasion. This dress was the last gift her mother gave her and the last dress bought in a store until long after she became an adult. As a young adult, she sewed her own dresses from feed and flour sacks, which companies made in different prints that women found appealing.[‡] The adjustment was small compared to what came next. Immediately after Asalee's death, Henry Lee refused to allow William Poole and Sarah visits with their grandchildren. Henry Lee forbade any contact until the Redds were erased from the lives of his children. He felt that his in-laws attached too many strings to their gifts, such as

[‡] Beginning in the late twenties, feed and flour sack fabric became a popular way to save money and still have fashionable dresses. Three yards of print cotton cost around sixty cents when purchased from Sears and Roebuck, and three yards of gingham dress material cost around forty cents. Three yards of dress-quality gingham used in Gingham Girl Flour sacks made by the George P. Plant Milling Company, however cost only the price of the flour. A dress could be made from two or three 100-pound bags of flour. See Karen Strike, "Feed Sack Fashions and Patterns of Depression Era America," March 2, 2017, *Flashbak*, https://flashbak.com/feed-sack-fashions-and-patterns-of-depression-era-america-374786/.

questions about their daughter's death.

Inas walked over a mile to school each way—and yes, barefooted, at least in the warm weather. All the children in the communities did this to save their shoes from wear and tear. Bertha accompanied Inas each day. Beatrice became more bitter about her situation. One morning she shouted at Bertha that she would never marry, and Bertha would be wise not to do so either. Relief showed up in the form of Mary Isabelle Bagwell—Henry Lee's longtime mistress. Mary Isabelle was a local girl born to William E. and Eleanor Bagwell in the Chestatee Community. She brought a son to the union, who was born in 1910. Most of the neighbors believed—and rightly so—that Lebur Calvin was Henry Lee's flesh-and-blood son. Inas always referred to him as her half-brother instead of her stepbrother. Lebur is listed as a Hawkins and as Henry Lee's son in the 1920 census. Inas became best friends with Lebur and would remain so until he died in 1966 from a head injury after falling out of a tree. Inas always claimed he was drinking on the day he died, but my mother told the story of his death like this: Lebur climbed a big oak in front of the Atlanta boarding house where he lived. When he was midway up the large tree, he sat on a limb and taunted anyone who pleaded with him to come down. When no one was expecting him to give up, he threw himself out of the tree. Lebur was rushed to the hospital, where he lived for a few days but eventually died from his head injury and internal injuries. Mother claimed he wasn't "right in the head" and hadn't been since he served in World War II. While researching for this book, I found Lebur's military registration card. His signature looks eerily similar to Inas's. There is little known about Lebur, though Inas was fond of talking about him as a boy. His wife is a witness listed on the registration card, so it is confirmed that he married. Lebur was fifty-six and penniless when he jumped from the tree. Inas paid for the burial expenses and laid his body to rest in her personal family plot.

Two years later in January 1968, my Granny Inas took me to see Lebur's mother Mary Isabelle—she was called "Bell"—in Roswell, Georgia. In the living room was an antique upright piano and an antique iron bed. Even at my age of ten, I understood that the two pieces of furniture reflected something of the young woman Mary Isabelle had been—much more than a stepmother or Henry Lee's mistress and second wife. Music was a luxury in her difficult life with Henry Lee. At the time I met her, she was very obese and wore a faded housedress that snapped up the front. The image of her being young, more than likely pretty, was hard to see. This woman had loved to play music in a time when women were often overlooked as artists of any kind. Bell looked at me standing by her bed and continued looking over at me during our visit, but I realized that she looked through me, past me, maybe to the place she was headed; maybe she saw her first son, Lebur, waiting. Her skin was tinged a grayish yellow, and it was obvious that no one came to visit or to care for her. My stomach clinched at the thought. I never understood why Inas insisted on taking me to visit her stepmother. Two weeks later, news came that Mary Isabelle had died at home in her bed. Inas always spoke of her with a tender kindness, as if some part of her understood the affair between Henry Lee and Mary Isabelle, as if this woman had no real choices when it came to Henry Lee. After all, he always got exactly what he wanted. As she had for Lebur, Inas paid for Mary Isabelle's burial and had her placed next to her first son in Inas's family plot.

The locals were not so compassionate toward Mary Isabelle and Henry Lee in Hightower. A rumor that Henry Lee killed Asalee so he could be with Mary Isabelle became the real explanation for Asalee's death. The community began showing their disapproval in a quiet but demanding way. The citizens of Forsyth County had proven numerous times over the years that they knew how to handle crimes committed among their communities with their own brand of justice. One would expect some level of loyalty toward a man who had helped clean the county of African Americans and even helped hang two of the communities' most reviled men, believed to be the brutal murderers and rapists of a young white woman. But a campaign to punish Henry Lee took place in the years after he brought Mary Isabelle into his house. No matter the subtle threats and warnings, Henry Lee dug in his feet and held on to the area that his family help settle. By this point, his parents and siblings had long moved away. Claiborn and Georgia lived near Dalton, Georgia.

The whole family, including Inas, went into the fields to pick cotton, not unlike other children on surrounding farms. What made their task unusual was the fact that Inas and her siblings never had to work in the fields before their mother died. This made attending school on a regular basis tough for all the children. Inas's tender hands cracked open and bled, then cracked open again day after day until leather-like calluses formed as she pulled the fluff of cotton from its sharp shell—the work of an adult. Henry Lee's disposition did not improve; if anything, it worsened, and living with him became a real challenge. He could no longer escape the hard times other families in the area were experiencing. These families had worked in Henry Lee's fields, picking his cotton before his wife died.

Those days were gone. Worse things were about to happen.

The first two decades of the twentieth century were known as the Progressive Era throughout the country. Most state governments, including Georgia, generated Progressive reforms. The areas of economics, social expectations and status, and morality went through major changes. This included prohibition (which involved laws against making, transporting, and selling alcohol) and a plea to farmers to grow crops other than the overall popular crop, cotton. The farmers didn't much care for the moral movement to outlaw liquor, and they cared even less for the suggestion of changing their crops. If cotton was providing a good living, why not continue to grow it? As a result of their choice, Georgia produced a record 2.8 million bales of cotton on 4.9 million acres in 1911. The boll weevil invaded four years later, reducing the crop by 29 percent during the years 1918–1924. The Great Depression began much earlier for Georgia farmers than for the rest of the country. So even if Henry Lee and his family hadn't been shunned, they, like everyone else in the area, would have fallen on hard times by 1918, three years after the death of Asalee.

In late summer 1918, Inas was nine years old. She worked in the cotton fields every day with Mary Isabelle and the rest of the children. Even little Stella Mae was there, working beside Inas and Bertha. The girls' fingers and palms were covered with tough calluses that no longer bled. Baby Mary, now four, played on the fringes of the field, and all the kids were careful to watch her. Mary Isabelle had a new son named Obar, whom she kept as close to her as possible. He was a little over a year old at picking time and a handful to watch. Like his mother, Obar grew up to be a musician—a very good one. Those humid, steamy days of picking cotton brought the children together with their stepmother Mary Isabelle. On rare occasions Henry Lee worked with them in the fields, but mostly he was gone. Inas was glad. She didn't care what he was doing. Clyde and Lebur found ways to get away from the fields as much as possible. The younger children looked up to Mary Isabelle, understanding that if not for her, their lives would be much harder. Inas learned to cook from her stepmother, but best of all she learned to sew. The act of a needle pushing through cloth calmed the young Inas and gave her a way of being useful and creative at the same time. Making stitches took her away from the painful reality of scarce food and hard labor. Sewing gave her a pleasure to look forward to on any given day. No one told her she was wasting time instead of helping the family like they did when she read books. At ten, Inas often thought of running away to find her big brother Elbert. The needle would push the thread in and out of the cloth as she worked, maybe on a dress for Mary, and she imagined how she would walk away from the farm, carrying her two dresses and shoes in a flour sack. Just walk, hiding in the ditch if Henry came looking, but knowing he probably wouldn't even look. This dream kept her working in the cotton fields, kept her planning a life that she prayed was possible: Elbert and her living in a small house, with her cooking for him, sewing his clothes. Deep down, even at this young age, Inas knew the whole fantasy was impossible.

One oppressively hot morning that summer, Inas went to the fields with the family as she had the whole month of August. Part of her could not understand why they even bothered to pick. The cotton was horrible because of the weevil. Henry Lee was going to lose everything sooner or later anyway. The whole family knew this. If not for Ernest, who shared what he earned working for the Fouts Brothers some twenty-five miles southwest of their farm, the family would have gone completely hungry. The Fouts Brothers worked for the Martin family and were known for their moonshine. Ernest placed himself right smack in the middle of this enterprise. There was one thing farmers couldn't do without in hard times, something that they would starve to have: liquor. Prohibition had allowed a lucrative underground business to form all over the country, but especially in Appalachia. Ernest had a secret career that could save his brothers and sisters who slaved in the fields.

The sun was nearly straight up in the sky, beating on the kids and Mary Isabelle. Dinnertime couldn't come soon enough, even if it was cold, hard biscuits and fried fatback leftovers from breakfast. Inas looked up and saw a thick cloud of black, oily smoke curling above the treetops.

"Looked like a calling-card from the devil himself," Granny said more than one time when telling this story to me.

"Bell," Inas called.

The family ran as hard as they could to the house and found it completely engulfed in orange flames. One of the boys, maybe Clyde, ran for Henry Lee. The other kids used buckets of water from the well, attempting to put out the fire. By the time Henry Lee returned home, the house had collapsed. Everything the family had burned. Any keepsakes of Asalee were gone. Granny's general thought was that someone, maybe all of Hightower, wanted to punish Henry Lee for what he did to Asalee. Other families must have seen the smoke billowing into the sky. Maybe it reminded them of the burning of homes and churches that belonged to the African Americans only a few years before as they fled with what belongings they could carry: the cleansing that Henry and his fellow vigilantes made happen. No one came to help. Henry Lee's family was left homeless.

It is not clear where the family stayed until they found a new home. Mary Isabelle's family lived in the nearby community of Chestatee, so surely her parents or some other relatives opened their home. Ultimately, Ernest came to the rescue of his family by purchasing a house in Seven Branches, Georgia. This home was built close to the Chattahoochee River on what is now Fouts Road, not far from what was called Martin's Ferry, popular with surrounding communities as a river crossing point at the turn of the century.[§] Fouts Road still exists today, but the river is no longer reachable due to an eight-foot wooden fence.

Inas moved from Forsyth County with only what she wore on her back, leaving her childhood hometown forever. The next time the family would venture back to the community would be to bury one of Henry Lee's daughters. With the move, neither Inas nor Lebur returned to school. Inas had made it through the fifth grade, better than many kids on farms. This new house on Fouts Road was the first and only

---

[§] Martin's Ferry, also known as Grogan's Ferry, was operated by Reuben Martin in the 1830s on the Chattahoochee River not far from Roswell, Georgia. The ferry consisted of a rope stretched across the river with bow and stern lines attached to it. The pressure of the current against the ferry moved it across the river. This ferry accommodated a horse and wagon. The toll for loaded wagons was sixty-two cents, and empty wagons were fifty cents. In the 1840s, Thomas Grogan took over the ferry, and by 1863, James Roswell King and Thomas Edward King—the owners of Ivy Mills—bought the land on the north side of the river, including the ferry site. Throughout generations, the ferry has been referred to as Martin's Ferry. Additional information can be found in the *Dunwoody Crier*.

home Henry Lee would own outright.

The 1920 census shows Henry Lee as head of household and Mary Isabelle as his wife.[**] Ernest, now twenty, along with Clyde, Bertha, Inas, Lebur, Stella, Mary, Obar, and a twenty-two-year-old laborer also lived on the farm. The one person missing in the census is bossy Beatrice. At that time, she was in Atlanta as a boarder on Ashby Street and working at the Filing Corp as a tile inspector. She wanted to make something of herself and get away from watching children. And so at age seventeen, Beatrice was on her own, supporting herself, and did not marry for a long while.

[**] There is no marriage certificate proving that Henry Lee and Mary Isabelle were married.

Stone 5
Death Keeps Showing Up

Henry Lee bounced back from the fire and devastation he experienced in Hightower. One family archive states he built a large barn with several stables and "sliding doors that rolled on tracks." Ernest must have footed the bill for this extravagance too. The family had a fresh start, despite Henry Lee's horrible choices, and became free of the baggage of rumors surrounding Asalee's death. Inas was finally able to answer an inquiry about her mother with the simple response, "She died from an accidental fall." Once again Henry Lee had dodged a bullet and come out on top. But if there is a hero in this story, it's Ernest. He saved his father and siblings from the fate of so many struggling families in the foothills of Appalachia: poverty.

The family's closest neighbors were Paul and Marcus Fouts, Ernest's bosses. The brothers answered to Henry Martin, who owned much of the land in the surrounding area. This enterprising group of young men had grown a lucrative moonshine business beyond anyone's imagination, and as long as the revenue men didn't get wind of the endeavor, prosperity would abound for Martin, the Fouts brothers, and their families. Their alliance was making money hand over fist. Bars—Inas called them taverns—opened in the basements of homes and were popular with the locals, who needed to unwind from the burdens placed on their shoulders, prohibition being one such malady. The Temperance Movement* had not succeeded in driving the liquor out of homes in Georgia—or anywhere in the country for that matter.

Paul and Marcus Fouts were transplants from Coal Mountain in Forsyth County, not too far from where Henry Lee had lived. The brothers' father had died when the youngest child, Corine, was three in 1907. Sigal, the oldest son, left the mountain and moved to Newtown, Georgia, married a young woman named Ethel, and had a baby daughter. Brothers Paul and Marcus soon followed, leaving Corine and their mother, Lydia, on the homeplace. By 1917, Paul and Marcus had moved into their own house on Fouts Road and decided to bring the remaining family. The family archive tells of Paul coming for Lydia and Corine. Two wagons were loaded with belongings. Corine, thirteen, drove one wagon and Lydia the other. Paul drove his truck, also loaded. Paul and Marcus are listed as farmers on the 1920 census—a safe occupation that did not attract attention.

In June 1920, Ernest married Corine. This seems a natural

---

* The Temperance Movement began in Georgia in the late 1820s but didn't really take off until 1908, and then it remained statewide until 1935. This time in Georgia's history began before and extended beyond national prohibition (1920–1933). In the beginning, the Georgia State Temperance Society met in tandem with the Baptist State Convention, so intertwined were the two groups. The Atlanta race riot of 1906 encouraged state lawmakers to enact prohibition. There was a common fear that African Americans who drank would cause issues, and white mobs often originated in bars and saloons. These were identified as causing the terror of the riot, thus necessitating strict laws against alcohol. See David M. Fahey, "Temperance Movement," March 10, 2003, *New Georgia Encyclopedia*, https://www.georgiaencyclopedia.org/articles/history-archaeology/temperance-movement.

choice for the two since Ernest was around Corine constantly and their romance flourished. Ernest was four years older than his new wife. On the couple's wedding day, Paul gave Corine one hundred dollars, a massive fortune to farmers of the time, for a nice outfit and a honeymoon. The couple's wedding night was spent in Atlanta's Majestic Hotel, one of the top three hotels in the city located on Peachtree Street. Ernest was living quite a different life from that of his childhood. He purchased land and an old house from Mr. Martin, property located on the corner of Fouts and Holcomb Bridge Road, for Corine and him to begin their life together. If Ernest believed from that minute forward that he would spend time building his family and not worrying about his brothers and sisters, he was sadly mistaken. He remained the true head of the Hawkins family for many years into his future.

There is little evidence that any of Henry Lee's extended family came to visit Newtown, but I have to believe he had contact with them. His parents Claiborn and Georgia had moved from the family home in Hightower sometime between 1900 and 1910, and landed in Calhoun, Georgia, off of Carter and Resaca Roads, sixty-one miles from Henry Lee—a long trip in those days. The couple had one grown daughter, Ida, living close by with her husband Oscar Owens and their children. With his family scattered across North Georgia, it would seem unlikely that Henry Lee remained close to his siblings. Yet there is proof that Inas knew her first cousins when she was grown. The family stayed in touch. Maybe they gathered on special occasions, and maybe they even had a family reunion or two.

The Chattahoochee River, within walking distance of the family's new farm, was the soft music that sang Inas to sleep at night in warm weather. The water lapped at the banks, and night birds called out to the moon. A litany of crickets chirped in the cooler air. And even though the flat land around the farm would flood in bad rain, she was enchanted with the wooded places and marshy banks. At eleven, with no real time to act like a kid, moments of solitude and nature were important, rare, and precious. Henry Lee—like most farmers—expected all the children old enough to handle a hoe to work in the fields and perform adult chores around the house. Bertha and Inas were in charge of the kitchen garden where most of the food for winter was grown. Later in life Inas would have only flower gardens that she worked late in the evening when the sun dipped behind the horizon. "Just for pleasure," she said. When given the chance, the two older sisters escaped outside to the river to skip rocks and break the rule of wading into the sometimes dangerous currents. Neither girl had the luxury of learning to swim, but they didn't care. The sisters tied their dresses around their waists, took off their shoes if they were wearing any, and waded in as far as was safe. Inas found happiness in the ebb and flow of nature and often shared this love with me when I was old enough. Visiting her flowerbeds was always a lovely treat with her descriptions. Butterflies would flit in and out of the bright blooms.

Long days spent in the fields picking corn, beans, and, in August, the godforsaken cotton toughened the children's spirits. Summer was more of a free time from continuous work. Sickness was not so prevalent. Not many folks came down ill in the hot months. Inas and Bertha helped Mary Isabelle can the food for winter, a welcome respite from the backbreaking field work. When the corn came in, harvesting it was an all-day event. Sometimes they would have shucking parties in front of the barn. Families from the community came to help. Shuckings were as good as birthday parties to Inas. Dozens upon dozens of ears of white sweet corn were piled taller than the kids and as big around as a large oak tree. The husks were pulled away and all the silks—the long, hair-like strands around the ear of corn—were removed. Lord help the kid who left a silk stuck on his or her ear of corn. The heat beat down on them as the day wore on, and clean ears were deposited on a large blanket. The women were in the kitchen blanching the cobs. Then they scraped and scooped the kernels into canning jars.

A good hour into the shucking process, the black flies would begin to buzz around the heads of the children, biting their bare skin with stinging fury. The higher the pile of husks and silks, the more black flies invaded. This was a bittersweet gathering. Inas found she could tolerate the irritating insects to have the fun of joking around, singing songs, and enjoying what should have been an unrelenting job.

For the midday meal, which they called "dinner," everyone was given a plate of hot, buttery, fried corn with homemade cornbread and a slice of fried fatback. Fried corn is cooked in a cast-iron frying pan with globs of bacon grease and a good amount of homemade butter—not good for one's heart, but in those days families worked so hard that they burned off the offending cholesterol. This process was repeated many times in the harvesting season at different farms in the form of bean-stringing and pea-shelling parties. Inas's favorite parties of the season took place when the fruit ripened. She liked peaches the best. They would pick the peaches from their small grove of trees and help skin and pit them. In return, a large pan of peach cobbler was placed on the outside table, each child was given a spoon, and they got to eat straight from the pan.

Often Inas would scald her mouth trying to get as much as she could before one of her dumb brothers got the most. Beautiful jars of apple butter, peach butter, and plum butter were canned each season. Henry Lee would barter with other farms and bring home pecans and black walnuts. Close to Halloween, the pumpkins were picked. Many were taken to market for selling, but Mary Isabelle always made pies and the kids made jack-o-lanterns, placing real candles in the hollowed-out shells. Parties for Halloween were always the best because the sweet desserts were plentiful. In November, the potatoes were ready. Inas's favorite was sweet potatoes. Mary Isabelle would set them on the hot coals in the woodstove and bake them. Often for supper they had hot, buttery sweet potatoes sprinkled with brown sugar. And always on Thanksgiving, Ernest killed two of the hens and brought them to Mary Isabelle for baking. She made sweet potato and pecan pies for desserts. Their hogs could be sold for good money, but they always kept enough back to feed the family, salting the meat and smoking it in the smokehouse. Inas loved smoked ham slices much better than the coveted hens the others liked so well. Bertha made biscuits the size of a cat's head, light and fluffy. Inas used the sorghum syrup liberally. Life could be good at times, and Inas tried to cling to those moments.

On March 29, 1921, the ground for the new crops and gardens were being planted. Inas and Bertha worked on the kitchen garden, planting green beans, yellow squash, cucumbers—for Bertha's famous sweet pickles—and Inas's rows of flowers. Mary Isabelle scolded her, saying flowers wouldn't put food in her belly, but this didn't bother Inas. The flowers gave her beauty, and she believed everyone needed a little pretty in their lives, even her daddy. The day was warm, almost hot, and the girls had fun while they worked. Supper was good if not plentiful. The beginning of spring put a strain on the last of the food "put up" for winter months. After cleaning the supper dishes, the kids went to bed. Inas and Bertha shared a bed in the back part of the house. Inas woke in the night to heat radiating off of Bertha's body.

"I'm sick, Inas," her sister said through chattering teeth. She shook so hard the bed moved.

"I'll go get Bell." Inas threw back her covers.

"No. I'll tell her in the morning. She's worn out after all that planting today. Let her sleep. Maybe the fever will break and I'll be better."

Inas went back to sleep.

The next morning, Dr. Brooks was called. He ordered Bertha be quarantined in a room alone. She had strep throat, and the illness could spread to all the people in the house. Mary Isabelle was sure that Inas would be the next one to come down sick, but somehow Inas was spared. Five days later on April 3, Bertha's fourteenth birthday, her fever broke and she seemed to get better. Inas baked her a chocolate cake, and Bertha ate a slice. The family's relief that Bertha was better was dashed a few days later when the fever returned. Dr. Brooks returned and diagnosed Bertha with rheumatic fever, one of the illnesses that claimed too many lives in that era.[†]

[†] Rheumatic fever can result from strep throat that is not treated. In the early 1920s, there weren't any antibiotics, so this infection reared its ugly head and caused the body to attack its own tissues, often resulting in heart disease. At the time, rheumatic fever was the leading cause of death in children ages 5 to 20 and second only to tuberculosis. See Edward F. Bland, MD, "Rheumatic fever: the way it was," *American Heart Association Journal*

Bertha remained in bed. Because Mary Isabelle followed the old ways—feed a cold, starve a fever—Bertha was barely fed, eating only broth and the occasional piece of bread. With all the people living in the house at the time and food harder to come by at that time of year, it must have been easy to use Bertha's food portions for the other children. Inas, who went in to visit her sister each morning and afternoon, always suspected Henry Lee was behind the scant rations given to Bertha.

"I'm so hungry, Ini," Bertha said, using her nickname for Inas, a name that would stick with her the rest of her life among her sisters. "I might be sick, but starving me isn't going to help me."

As the months passed, Inas brought her precious slice of fried ham from her breakfast each morning and part of her sliced fatback each evening to Bertha, who tore into the meat, chewing with such intent that Inas was consumed with guilt for not bringing her food sooner. If this helped Bertha get better, Inas knew it was a small sacrifice to be a little hungry.

Despite regaining some of her appetite, Bertha didn't get stronger, and sometimes she was weaker. Walking across the room was a chore and took every ounce of energy she owned. Inas missed walking to the river with Bertha. She missed her company in the kitchen and in the fields. Each evening Inas told Bertha stories about the younger siblings. Often they broke into loud laughter, causing Mary Isabelle to come in and warn Inas of exhausting her sister. Inas read to Bertha from any available books. Surely they were like any pair of teenage sisters, talking about things like boys. Inas grew closer to Lebur, too,

---

76/6 (December 1987), http://circ.ahajournals.org/content/circulationaha/76/6/1190.full.pdf.

and loved the little ones, Stella, Mary, and Obar. She cherished every morning when she looked in on Bertha and saw her smile.

Christmas came, and Bertha was too sick to come to the table for the dinner of baked ham, dressing, candied yams, pecan pie, and cornbread. There were no stockings hung at the hearth of the Hawkins house. Even so, Mary Isabelle made sure each child received a piece of fruit, a true treat. Inas envied oranges and would trade her apple for one. Henry Lee saw holidays like Christmas as a waste of time. Because of his attitude and everything that happened with her sister, this holiday was always hard for Inas. On New Year's Eve of 1921, Inas rung in the New Year with Bertha, feeling certain that the year of 1922 would be a good one. They laughed and talked until Bertha drifted off to sleep with Inas right beside her. She harbored hope and believed her sister would become well.

In the early morning hours of January 19, Inas woke from a deep sleep, thinking someone had called her name. The room was freezing, and smoke came from her mouth when she took a breath. The wood fire had gone out. Her bare feet touched the hardwood floors and a shiver worked through her body. When she pushed the door open to Bertha's room, she whispered, "Bertha, did you call me?"

Her sister didn't answer, so she tiptoed to the side of the bed and touched Bertha's head, which felt warm but not hot. She gave Bertha a gentle shake, but she didn't stir. Inas went back to bed, hopeful Bertha was getting better.

After daylight, Mary Isabelle notice a distinct change in Bertha's coloring, a graying of her skin. Her eyes were sunken. Breathing was labored. She called Dr. Brooks. At age fourteen, Bertha took her last breath at 7:00 pm that evening with Inas sitting beside her.

Bertha was buried the next morning in Friendship Baptist Church Cemetery, next to her mother. Later, a large stone was erected at the head of her grave—a more elaborate and ornate stone than Asalee's.

Inas always felt like a part of her died along with Bertha, and she never quite got over losing her. "Some souls aren't meant to walk the earth for long, but I believe Bertha should have lived to be an old woman," Inas said multiple times. This beautiful girl was deeply missed by her brothers and sisters.

The awful family tragedies were not over. On April 22, Mary Isabelle gave birth to a daughter who never took a breath. The child was not given a name on her death certificate, and the grave has not been found. The only enlightening information on the death certificate was the word "stillborn."

Stone 6
The Child without a Story

Inas was closemouthed about how she met JD Lord, my grandfather. In the 1920 census, JD shows up as age twelve and is listed as a farm laborer. He was born in the Newtown, Georgia, area that neighbored Seven Branches. His family is recorded as living in the Newtown/Roswell community from the early 1800s.

Inas must have met JD at Mt. Pisgah Methodist Church, where both families attended services. JD's father laid the brick for the original chapel, which still stands today, on Nesbitt Ferry Road near Roswell. This is where Inas would bury family members Lebur and Mary Isabelle in the future. The Hawkinses populated many family plots in this cemetery. Both the Hawkinses and the Lords still live in the Newtown area today.

By 1924 Inas, fifteen, had grown close to JD, seventeen. When I was a little girl and so wanted to believe in happily-ever-after stories, I imagined my grandparents meeting at high school, maybe at a dance. I had no idea that neither Inas nor JD had gone to school past the fifth grade. I imagined tall, lanky JD, with big ears, sheepishly dropping by Henry Lee's house to court Inas. They must have sat on the front steps and talked. Would they have dreamed about a life together? Both lived hardscrabble lives helping their families survive. Maybe JD stole a kiss when he was sure Inas's brothers and father were nowhere nearby. JD took Inas home to meet his mother, Lizzie. Inas always spoke of her fondly.

JD was the oldest of two children belonging to Jacob Webb Lord and Nancy Elizabeth (Lizzie) Sims. Jacob Webb was fifty-four when he married thirty-nine-year-old Lizzie Sims on October 23, 1903. There is a color photo of Lizzie, Jacob Webb, and Maggie—JD's younger sister. Jacob Webb is seated in front of his wife and daughter. His hair is pure white, and he wears a white beard that reaches his belt. Lizzie has golden-brown hair put up on her head and isn't smiling, but Maggie wears a large smile.

In October 1924, Inas was fully in charge of the younger kids—Mary and Obar. Eleven-year-old Stella helped out when she was there, but often she could be found at Ernest's house, helping Corine. Part of Inas's duties were to sew and mend the clothes belonging to the family. With experience, she became quite good, and every chance she got she embroidered intricate flowers, birds, and trees. She must have made Mary's school dresses from the flour sacks covered in floral print and added delicate touches where she could, like embroidery or lace around the collars and sleeves. Mary must have looked up to Inas and grown close to her, especially after Bertha died. I have to believe Inas told her stories of Asalee and Elbert, taught her to sew and cook, calmed her fears. Maybe she took her on walks to the river, where they watched the blue heron nest in the tall, skinny trees.

In the first week of October, Mary came down with a sore throat that grew progressively worse, including a headache and high fever. Dr. Brooks was called, and Mary was diagnosed with strep throat that once again turned into rheumatic fever and caused her to have a heart condition. Unlike Bertha's long bout with the illness, Mary's sickness ended after only two months. Maybe it was her younger age, or by this time perhaps the family was struggling to keep food on the table because of cotton prices. Ernest helped and no one starved, but he too had a family to care for and couldn't put his whole focus on his extended family. Often Inas told of having only cornbread and fried fatback for dinner while the best of the food went to the males in the house, the reasoning being that they worked in the fields and had to keep their health. Children were always last on the list in Inas's home.

Mary died on December 8, 1924, at 10:00 am. Dr. Brooks was in attendance each day from December 1 through December 8 due to complications caused by mitral regurgitation of the heart. Mary took her last breath on the morning of December 8 with her family around her. Inas must have been there with her, but she never talked about this death like she did others.

Mary was buried beside Bertha the next day. A small two-foot headstone was eventually placed by the two large, ornate markers belonging to Asalee and Bertha. There was no date of birth or death on Mary's marker, only the years she lived, and her middle initial was different: an L instead of an A for Alice.

When I stood in front of the three stones at this family plot ninety-three years after Mary's death, I asked myself who bought these markers. Did the Redds pay for Asalee's and Bertha's? Or did Henry Lee pay for all three, but money was tight when Mary Alice died? Henry Lee didn't seem like the type to buy an elaborate stone for his wife or daughter. The few stories that remain prove quite the opposite. By all indications, he never even bothered to legally marry his second wife, Mary Isabelle, which would have been a scandal. And how had Henry

Lee felt about Mary Alice? After all, she was a baby left motherless because of him. Did he feel guilt? His past actions would suggest that he didn't waste time on empathy or guilt. Without sounding too harsh, I find it hard to believe Henry Lee loved anyone. I'm not sure he knew how. Was Mary Alice designated a tiny stone because the Redds were no longer a part of their grandchildren's lives and did not know Mary Alice well? Were they at the funeral? Why would Inas keep Mary a secret? Why does she not show up in the family tree? No one will ever know Mary's complete story. Did she like vegetables? Was she kind? What color was her hair? Did she like school? Sometimes knowing part of the truth is much worse than not knowing anything at all.

Part Three

Ann

Stone 7
A Baby Is Born

November 9, 1996

Five years ago today, I met Jack, my boyfriend. In many ways, we have settled into an old married couple. We have a blended family, including my three daughters and his son. Our friends take our relationship for granted and forget that we are not married. I'm afraid. Part of me wants to make our relationship official with a big wedding and party, but the other part—who struggles to keep her independence after her first marriage—never wants to be married again.

Jack hasn't mentioned our five-year anniversary. His romantic side is one of the reasons I am so drawn to him. He always remembers important dates without silly hints. So if he forgets this time, I will have to cut him a break. I have a nice dinner planned. The kids were supposed to stay with their other parents this weekend, but at the last minute they decided to be home. The more the merrier. We will sit down at the dining room table—candles and music—and eat like a real family. My eighteen-year-old daughter, Cassey, recently moved into her own apartment with roommates. She is taking a year off from school before going away to college in New York City. She too will join us for dinner, seeing how her cupboard is bare. (My oldest daughter Melissa is managing a home of her own.) This day is not turning out like I thought it would. Yet good things have been known to happen on the craziest days.

A knock sounds at the door. There is a movement behind

me. I glance back and see Stephen with his father's video camera.

"Your dad wouldn't like you using his camera." I notice the red light blinking. The boy is recording me.

Another insistent knock. I give the camera a glare and throw open the door. Jack stands in front of me dressed in his three-piece suit, complete with a tie. Stephen laughs behind me. Beth stands in the door of the kitchen smiling from ear to ear. Jack pushes a large bunch of peach-color roses, my favorite, at me.

"May I come in?"

I take the flowers and look at him as if he has lost his mind. "You live here." My attire is gray sweatpants and an oversized green sweatshirt. My long hair is pulled up in a ponytail, and I'm not wearing a bit of makeup.

The red light on the video camera is still blinking. Jack stands in front of me and drops to one knee.

My world stands still.

"Ann, will you marry me? I have talked to Beth, Stephen, and Cassey. They agree it is high time we make this legal."

Stephen and Beth nod. Tears of happiness spring into my eyes. All the worry of making this decision falls away.

"Yes." Nothing has ever felt so right.

After the excitement settles, while I'm checking on dinner, I call Mother.

"Hello." She answers on the fourth ring.

"Mother, I have some news." I say a silent prayer that she doesn't react badly.

"What has happened?" She sounds out of breath. Why is it she never thinks there is good news?

"Something wonderful." I rush on talking so she can't interject negativity. "Jack asked me to marry him and I said yes."

There is silence.

I keep talking to fill the space. "We are planning the wedding over dinner tonight. I'm thinking spring. I always wanted a spring wedding."

"This is your second marriage, Ann. You aren't supposed to make a big deal."

The joy of the night deflates. "I can do what I want, Mother."

"You always have." And she hangs up the phone.

Jack and I are married on May 3, 1997, in a church ceremony that my daughters plan, even down to helping pick out my wedding dress. Finally, at the age of forty, I have a real wedding.

Mother stands beside me in photos. I hold her hand, her fingers interlaced with mine. When I look at these photos, I almost believe we are a normal mother and daughter, that we are happy, that we share secrets and laugh.

August 29, 1999, 4:20 am

Pain rips across my back and around to my stomach. I jerk awake and wait for it to pass. Jack is asleep beside me, and the house is silent. I am four days overdue, and each day has stretched out like a year. Beth will turn sixteen tomorrow, and her one wish is that the new baby will not be born on her birthday. It seems like she may get her request. I keep up with the time. Fifteen minutes have gone by without further discomfort. Maybe the pain was just a cruel trick to make me believe

I was actually going to give birth. But as the digital clock flips to 4:40, pain builds in my back and rushes over my stomach again. I breathe through it, happy to see the end. I'm not thinking about how this pregnancy has been high-risk, with many unforeseen complications. Neither am I thinking about my age and how it may change delivery times. I just want to have my baby girl.

When the pains increase to fifteen minutes apart around 5:00, I wake Jack. "It's time to go to the hospital." I make a phone call to Cassey, and we are on our way. I decide not to wake Mother so early in the morning.

Beth and Stephen sit blurry-eyed in the back of our van. Jack runs all the traffic lights, even though I assure him there is no need. We arrive at the Women's Center, where Cassey meets us in the lobby. Pains are coming every five minutes now and have become intense. My labor nurse tells me to walk up and down the halls. I look at her like she has lost her mind but give it a try. The pains grow to three minutes apart, but I am only dilated at two centimeters. Cassey, Beth, Stephen, and Melissa—my oldest daughter—come in for a quick visit.

"Are you hurting, Mom?" Cassey asks.

Truly, I want to tear out her eyes for asking such a question, but I don't want to scar her for life, make her never want to have children. She is my worrywart.

Melissa, who has two children of her own, rolls her eyes. "Yes. She is hurting."

"I need one of you to call your grandmother. She will be upset if you don't."

Beth shakes her head. "Not me."

A pain grips me, and I grab the wall closest to me and try not to groan too loud.

"Let's go. We'll be in the lobby, Mom." Cassey heads for the big double doors.

"Call your grandmother." I say after them. Not one of them volunteers, but I assume they will. They find it hard to be around Mother. She is always disagreeable, and they hate how she treats me.

The pains begin to move through me every two minutes, but I'm only dilated at five. "Not long," the labor nurse says after an exam. "How about some more walking?"

"I don't think I can." The pains are much worse than with my other three pregnancies. "I'm going to sit in this rocker." On the wall is a painting of the ocean. I think of St. Simon's, a barrier island off the Georgia coast. I sit on the edge of the rocker and rock as I stare at the painting. The crashing waves sound in my head, and I can see the tall lighthouse. With every pain, I rock harder and breathe deep. What seems like less than an hour is two hours.

The labor nurse comes in and does another exam. "We have eight. Time to go to your room."

In the Women's Center, I will give birth in the same room where the baby and I will remain for two nights. "Sounds good to me."

After we are settled, my water breaks. The labor nurse is stationed at my head and the midwife stands at the foot of the bed. "It's time," says the labor nurse.

Now the pains are coming one after another, one long continuous stabbing.

"Push," the midwife orders, a calm tone in her heavy Jamaican accent.

As if I need anyone to tell me this. My body is acting on its own.

On the fifth push, my body loses all its energy. My three girls came quicker than this little one.

The labor nurse leans over and whispers, "We are the same age. What were you thinking?" And this is the perfect thing to say to me. She acknowledges my effort, my age, and the months it took to get here.

I give her a weak smile. "I don't know."

The phone begins to ring close to my head.

Jack, a person who has never been able to let a phone just ring, answers it. "Hello."

A horrible pain pushes through my body and a scream—one of the first I've uttered—slides out.

"I'm sorry, Jeanette. One of the girls was supposed to call you."

Again I scream. This scream is as much for the fact that Mother has called my room complaining while I am delivering as it is for my pain and effort.

"I have to hang up, Jeanette. Ann is having the baby. I can't listen." Jack places the phone in the cradle.

I push one last time, and the relief of release moves through me. One wiggle and the midwife holds a baby, a beautiful baby girl.

Ella Jennifer Hite, named after Jack's mom and because of my passion for Ella Fitzgerald's music, is born at 11:26 am. She weighs nine pounds and three ounces. In a matter of minutes, she is surrounded by her sisters and brother. Her dad stands close to my right. Mother will not come to see her new granddaughter for two weeks, claiming she wasn't wanted at the hospital. But in reality, it is my happiness that puts her off. She knows my life is becoming everything she ever wanted and didn't manage to have for herself.

That night, I can't sleep for looking at Ella cuddled in the crook of my arm. Beside us on a cot sleeps her daddy, who refuses to leave us alone. We are a family. One big blended family.

Stone 8
A Mother's Love, Spring 2003

Mother doesn't love me. This knowledge runs through my mind each time she acts out, each time she asks me to cross the line drawn in the sand at my feet, placed there to protect me. Today is no different. I listen to my answering machine.

"Jack, this is Mom. Jeanette has called me, begging for money. I don't know what to do. The money she wants is a lot. I don't mind helping, but I want to see what Ann thinks." The phone clicks away from the voice of my husband's mother, and the machine moves on to the next call.

"Ann, Ann. Are you there. I need money. I need you to give me some money." I grip the kitchen counter to keep from crumpling to the floor. Horrible, death-gripping guilt tightens my chest. I want to call her back. And I don't want to call her. I am split in half. I am two people: a woman struggling with her mentally ill mother and a young girl who needs to please her mother. During my recent visit, my therapist gave me permission, suggested—*insisted*—I give myself a vacation from Mother. Two weeks with no communication. This is the worst vacation I have ever taken. But in reality, except for these phone calls I am happy, content. This is my dirty secret. I am relieved not to make her decisions. Not to have to persuade her to keep her doctor's appointments. When I'm forced to see her, I lose all resolve. I am the ten-year-old in the bed beside hers. I am the teenager taking the life-threatening beatings from her. And this person, this child, isn't able to cope with her demands, to stand up to her and say no. I cannot be around her.

I am fully aware that my mother is dying. Again, another secret. She wants to die, has wanted to die since she left a twenty-two-page suicide note for me when I was thirteen and belittled me for running to the neighbors for help. Now, once again, she threatens to use her means, her own body, to destroy herself by not following her doctor's orders. She refuses to go for dialysis treatments for a week at a time. She doesn't follow her strict diet but instead drinks gallons of buttermilk and eats nothing but containers of strawberries. No balance. Two weeks ago Jack found her collapsed on the bathroom floor as a result of her self-abuse. She was taken to the hospital, where it became evident to the doctor that she wasn't in her right mind to care for herself. This episode finally brought Jack to a place where he said no more. He realized if we continue to "help" Mother, we will aid her in dying. At least this is what I hope he realizes. He too is guilt ridden.

I present her with a list of state and government agencies that will help her get to and from her treatments. They will make sure she is eating healthy and gets her medicine. She refuses. The hospital insists I have Mother committed since she refuses help. I almost agree, but there is a catch. She is no different now than she was when she was raising me, abusing me, and deemed competent by the Division of Family and Children Services. And my younger brother Jeff is the only person she trusts or wants to make her decisions. He just happens to be out of the picture, off the map, disappeared, even though I suspect Mother knows where he is and what he is doing.

Mother and I don't agree when it comes to Jeff. We never have. She thinks he has no drug problem. I know he is addicted to meth and is an alcoholic. We do not discuss her love of prescription drugs, her self-medication to control her bipolar episodes. Two years ago I set boundaries, and she took this as a sign of my hate for both Jeff and her. For two years we didn't speak more than ten words until she needed the treatments. No, committing my mother would be wrong. I give the hospital Jeff's number and explain the situation, see the judgement on the nurse's face. Judgement or not, I can't put her away. It can't be me.

I am alone in the decision to walk away. Judgement and disbelief show in most people's eyes, even Jack's on most days. They do not understand why and how I can turn my back on my mother. They don't accept that I'm not out to hurt her, to punish her for all that she has done. I'm simply powerless to save a mother who doesn't want to be saved. I understand their confusion. I wish I could be one of these "normal" people with a mother I will miss to the bone when she is gone. I would give anything to be in a good relationship with Mother. I keep secrets buried inside. Not even my children—*especially* not my children—know the full extent of what I have witnessed and walked through. Sometimes I don't think I know. But still, this is not why I have turned away. I love Mother so deeply it hurts. She doesn't love me on her worst days and barely tolerates me on her best. We have spent a lifetime dancing between those two emotions with only rare occasions when a light shines on us and we communicate. No one knows how my very presence makes her resentful and angry. No one knows how even now as a grown woman I yearn to curl beside her, listen to her heartbeat, and have her accept me for who I am.

I love my mother too much to say she has been a bad parent. I love her too much to aid her in dying. I will have no part in her death even if she is miserable. I'm sorry.

Part Four

Inas Hawkins Lord (Loyd)

Stone 9
Death of a New Mother

Throughout little Mary's sickness, Inas was present and probably helped care for her sister once the danger of catching the disease had passed. And JD must have visited Inas and worried over her exposure to the illness. By this point in their relationship, the couple was in love, or at least thought they were. There are no stories of how JD courted Inas, but JD Lord and Inas Hawkins married on March 15, 1925, at the Roswell City Courthouse.

Inas never used her husband's real name in front of her daughter, Jeanette—my mother. If he was mentioned in one of Inas's stories, he appeared as an insignificant side character. One photo exists today of the couple: their wedding photo, featuring the two of them standing near Henry Lee's Model T. Inas shared this photo with Jeanette when she was in her sixties. Two by three inches, the picture was bent with torn corners. Jeanette promptly had it restored and made copies for Jeff and me. Upon placing the new eight-by-ten photo in my hand, she said, "My father died when I was five. I can still remember his smile and soft voice."

This man or boy of seventeen looked so much like my brother I couldn't speak. They could have been twins. In the picture JD sported a Scott Fitzgerald haircut and wore a white shirt tucked into what looked like dress pants and a light-colored tie. His smile was infectious, and looking at him I could see why Mother remembered his smile. My brother has JD's large ears, and noticing this made me laugh.

Inas stood just at JD's shoulder. Like JD, she wore a roaring twenties haircut, short just under her ear and combed dramatically to the side. Her dress was dark, with other details hidden by a large bush. Her expression was one of seriousness even on her wedding day. There was no smile. Her eyes looked tired and lacked any spark of hope. Maybe she still felt sadness over her most recent loss. Maybe she felt helpless or responsible for things no one could have changed. The expression made me think she had accepted that her life would be what it would be, and her hands were tied to do anything to change it. Inas was sixteen when she married. The photo at least revealed a happy young man, marrying his true love. No matter what took place in the future, his initial happiness was recorded, and for this I am thankful.

Where Inas and JD lived after they married is blurry at best. I have to guess they settled close to one of the families, maybe with JD's people. They were a very young couple. Inas often talked about her mother-in-law, Lizzie, who gave Inas a black ladder-back chair to begin "housekeeping." Inas's stories about this time in her life suggested that she was happy and content. Maybe she was even developing a bond with Lizzie as a mother figure. But once again, Inas's life was turned inside out. On April 13, 1925, in late afternoon, Inas and Lizzie walked down the road together at a leisurely pace, talking with each other. Inas was enjoying the conversation, but then Lizzie stopped speaking in the middle of a sentence and gave her an odd look. She fell back into a ditch and stared into the sky.

Inas screamed her mother-in-law's name, but Lizzie didn't respond. She was quite still and continued to stare off into space. Inas knelt down and found that her mother-in-law wasn't breathing. She was alone on a country road with Lizzie, who had died. Did she cry? Did she keep screaming? Somehow I can't imagine the young woman in the wedding photo going into hysterics. I see her calmly running to a nearby house for help.

Lizzie Sims Lord's death certificate states that she died instantly of a cerebral hemorrhage. Her son JD signed the death certificate, and his address at the time was Doraville, Georgia. Lizzie's personal information on the certificate is left blank, suggesting JD didn't know his grandparents on the Sims side. Later, I would find not only my paternal great-grandparents' names, James F. and Mary Sims, but also their graves in the nearby town of Dunwoody.

When Inas told the story of Lizzie's death, she never mentioned JD. I would imagine he was the person she ran to when Lizzie collapsed. Was it so painful to admit she needed him, sought out her husband? Who was he that she couldn't bring herself to mention his signing off on the death certificate? Dr. Brooks once again was the attending doctor. Inas had lost another person close to her.

Stone 10
The Christmas Birth

On Tuesday, October 29, 1929, Wall Street crashed and the whole country, teetering on economic disaster, plunged headfirst into the Great Depression. Appalachia and its foothills had already felt the Depression in the early twenties. Now the rest of the United States was falling apart. As people lost everything they had—money, jobs, homes, and the privilege of good meals—the dust bowl began to make things even worse in the plains.

When we talked about that time once, Granny remarked, "It was like God was punishing everyone for no good reason. Like it was the end of the world."

Cardboard jungles appeared in every community. Families were asked to believe that all would be well as their worlds fell apart. Those living in Newtown, Georgia, had more sense than to place those beliefs, wishes, and dreams in something they knew was pie in the sky. They hunkered down just like always and prepared to come out on the other side.

Each person's story has a root system that, when examined, unearths more questions than answers. The story of my mother Jeanette's decline, her mental instability, and her bipolar episodes can be traced back to Inas and JD's history. We all leave a roadmap into our past, and my mother is no different. Jeanette Mildred Lord was born December 24, 1929, just over the Dekalb County line outside of Newtown in a place called Shallow Ford. No baby photos of Jeanette exist, but what Inas possessed was a series of images burned into her memory, a story told often—what my brother and I would call the family's urban legend number one. That's not to say the story of Jeanette's birth wasn't true, only that it grew bigger and fuller with each telling.

Inas and JD lived in a small one-room house with a fireplace that was the centerpiece of the room. There was a wood-burning cookstove in the kitchen along with a pie safe cupboard where they stored food to consume later. Inas had no refrigerator and depended on smoked meats because they wouldn't ruin. The couple owned a rope bed with a corn-husk mattress, a small table with two chairs, and the black ladder-back chair given to Inas by Lizzie when the couple married. By the late fall of 1929, Inas and JD had been married almost five years. In their time together, JD had lost his mother and father. Finally, something wonderful was taking place. The couple would have their first child in the upcoming spring: late March or early April. Christmas was almost upon them. As I mentioned earlier, Inas never was fond of the holiday in my years with her. She never smiled. She never got excited about finding or buying gifts. All of her actions were implemented with a show of duty. This was what was expected of her. What would people say if she refused to buy gifts? If she opened a gift to herself, she didn't smile and thank the giver. Instead, she warned of spending too much money. Yet Inas was always generous with the gifts she bought, though it looked as if she did not enjoy being the gift-bearer. Maybe she felt this way because Mary Alice had died two weeks before Christmas. Maybe because Asalee had died and the joy of holidays was ruined by Henry Lee. Maybe because she feared if one enjoyed something, anything, too much, she was likely to lose it.

In her telling of the Christmas of 1929, Inas never mentioned JD. There was no indication that he was around when the events took place, even though I would like to think my grandfather was a character in the script. Christmas Eve turned cold, and Inas had to feed the fireplace to warm the tiny house. In her stories, there was no indication that she planned to visit Henry Lee or Ernest for the holiday. Sometime in the evening, pains rushed across her back, meeting around her stomach. Figuring she had eaten something that upset her stomach, she did not worry. At this part of the story, I now have to assume JD was there—someone had to be—because the doctor was summoned to the house. There were no phones in this rural area. Dr. Brooks, the same doctor who attended Bertha, Mary Alice, and Lizzie's deaths, now helped Inas give birth in her sixth month of pregnancy, three months too early.

After a difficult labor, Dr. Brooks pulled Jeanette feetfirst into the world. He took one look at this baby girl and said to Inas, "No need to get attached. This one should be thrown on the trash heap out back. She won't live until morning. She is too early." It sounds harsh, but he was simply speaking a deadly truth of the times. In most families, one more mouth to feed could make the difference between keeping one's farm or being homeless. And a child born as early as Jeanette could cost her parents their livelihood in medical expenses.

Rage flowed through Inas with the suggestion that she throw away her living, breathing daughter. Her losses had been too high. Fighting for her baby seemed the only way to fight back, to live, to fool the specter of Death. Her fearless attitude flared at Dr. Brooks. "You can leave now. I will not get rid of my baby. You're not needed here anymore."

What Inas did not know in those months after Jeanette's

traumatic entry was that her child's hip had been dislocated during the birth and would cause her a lifetime of trouble.

After cleaning her baby, which weighed less than a "a good-size baking potato," Inas wrapped Jeanette in a blanket she had made from a flour sack. She had also used it to sew a layette of gowns and diapers. Later, Inas would sew intricate dresses with smocking and tatting, a durable lace made with a series of knots and loops.

That Christmas Eve night, bricks were heated in the fireplace so the tiny infant with no fingernails or toenails, ears so thin they looked transparent—a baby so small she fit in the palm of Inas's petite hand—could be placed in the middle for warmth. Inas fed Jeanette pumped breast milk through an eyedropper, instantly becoming a twenty-year-old mother determined to save her baby. In one version of the story, Inas said caring for her tiny daughter wasn't so different from looking after a litter of puppies that the mama refused to feed.

Jeanette grew and thrived through the winter months. Inas didn't let her guard down, but she sighed with relief when Jeanette reached her original birth month happy and growing. This baby daughter would make it.*

More than once that winter, Inas denied visitors entry into her small house to see the baby. Her dedication to protect Jeanette from sickness was evident. She would not lose this child

* In the 1920s, infant mortality rates before age one were as high as one in ten in rural areas. Babies died of diarrhea, pneumonia, acute bronchitis, and other infectious diseases. Incubators were a source of amazement to the medical community, and few doctors believed they would work. It was 1960 before the first neonatal unit would open. Additionally, bacteria caused up to 40 percent of maternal deaths. Childbearing was a dangerous part of life in this time.

like she lost Bertha and Mary.

Jeanette was a Christmas miracle, and her story always accompanied, and sometimes outweighed, the original Christmas story of Jesus' birth in the manager. No matter what took place throughout the years, Inas always viewed Jeanette as her true gift. She was wholly devoted to this child and later the woman Jeanette would become.

Stone 11
A Mule Meaner than Him

After one of Granny's monthly visits to my great-aunt Stella's house in Roswell, Georgia, she took a detour on Holcomb Bridge Road, a narrow, two-lane rural route that ran through the middle of nothing but country—mostly woods with a tar-papered house here and there that stood on stacked field stones, looking as if I could push them off onto the ground. Granny turned onto Fouts Road and pointed at a long house with a porch that wrapped around it. I caught glimpses of the river. "Here is the old homeplace," she said. The house was exactly how she described in her stories. I wanted to stop, walk through it, find Bertha's room. But she kept driving, staring at the road.

In 1930, Henry Lee and Mary Isabelle were living in the Jones Bridge Road area not far from the house on the river. Eleven-year-old Obar, the couple's youngest son, was the only child left in the household by that time. There are no stories of why Henry Lee left the home that was mortgage free in 1920. Did he, like so many, get a mortgage on his place and lose it? Ernest and his growing family still lived in the same home on Fouts Road by the river. Inas told a story that when the Depression hit, Ernest began to buy land from farmers who couldn't pay their loans and rented it back to them. This saved the farmers from being homeless in a time when so many had suffered that fate, and it also gave him a profit. One of the family archives states, "There was in all about a hundred and twenty acres up and down both sides of Holcomb Bridge and Scott Road that Daddy Ernest owned." Could Ernest have bought the farm back from his father to prevent its loss? Or did Ernest have his father move to a smaller farm he had acquired since the family had shrunk?

No stories of Henry Lee's life in Newtown were preserved. Census records show that in 1930 Henry Lee and Mary Isabelle owned a radio. This was a luxury at the time, so apparently their situation wasn't desperate. One story of Henry Lee's death shows up in the family archive. In early April 1932, he was turning the ground in one of his fields with a listing plow pulled by a "mean" mule. Somehow the mule kicked Henry Lee in the head. The tale claims he died from the blow after lingering in the hospital for days. Of course, there is an echo in his death of how Asalee died—a blow to the head.

Henry Lee's death certificate, however, tells a much different story. On April 3, 1932, Henry Lee was taken to St. Joseph's Hospital in Atlanta. He remained there until April 7, when he died of acute nephritis, determined by blood tests performed at the hospital. Acute nephritis is an infection of the kidney. There are different types, but a single type is not specified on the death certificate. The most common nephritis that causes death is E. coli infection. This is still deadly to patients today, even though we have developed strong antibiotics.

Henry Lee was dead at age fifty-six. Maybe the mule story began because he really was kicked by the mule before he got the infection. Or maybe it was a story Ernest told his kids: *Your grandfather was so mean that it took a mule meaner than him to kill him.* There is no answer. But Henry Lee's reputation was well known, and people may have thought a man like that couldn't die of a kidney infection.

Inas never spoke to me about her father's death. Did she see him at the hospital? By that time, she had a second daughter, so she was caring for two small children. Surely she attended the funeral. Henry Lee was buried in Friendship Baptist Cemetery on the opposite end of the large graveyard from his wife Asalee and their daughters, Bertha and Mary. He was buried by his baby son, Glinn, who had died in 1907. There was still room in Asalee's plot, so the placement of their graves speaks volumes.

What became of Mary Isabelle, who was thirty-nine when Henry Lee died? Did she stay on at the rented farm for a while? Did she go home to the community of Chesatee? Did her son Lebur from her first marriage come home to help? According to his military registration card, he was married and living in Atlanta by 1940, so he would not have been far away. By the time Inas buried Mary Isabelle in her plot in 1968, Mary Isabelle's surname had changed to Jenkins. I can hope that Mary Isabelle had a better life with her new husband.

Henry Lee's death left Ernest as the head of the Hawkins family. Ernest and his wife Corine now had three daughters: Jewel, Doris, and their youngest, Audrey, who was only two months younger than Jeanette. Ernest had built his family a larger, more stylish six-room house with a wide wraparound porch. There was a full second floor. In the Depression, Corine furnished the living room with a store-bought sofa set and an upright piano. Each room had a working fireplace, and the kids were expected to keep the wood stacked in each of the rooms during the cold weather.

Ernest dug a well across Fouts Road from his house, where he placed a windmill that was used to pump water into a big tank. Pipes ran under the road to the house, and a bathroom and kitchen sink were added. The water was heated in the tank of the woodstove and used for washing dishes and taking baths. He also installed a Delco system that pumped water to supply electricity for lights. A kerosene refrigerator was installed as well. By the area's standard, Ernest was a wealthy man. He was flourishing, and owning Henry Lee's property, including the house and barn, only bettered his means further. All around Ernest were farmers whose farms he owned. According to Inas, he had no problem using his status to his advantage when he needed something.

Henry Lee made many choices that painted him as a man who didn't hold his family as precious. He harbored a strong sense of hate for those who were different from him. I have to wonder what he thought of his three-year-old granddaughter, Jeanette, who couldn't walk because of her missing hip socket; Inas was told that either Jeanette had been born without a hip socket because of her premature birth or it had dissolved. Did Henry Lee give her the time of day? Did he soften before his death? Or did he fully earn his reputation as the man who got killed by a mule meaner than him?

Stone 12
Not a Drop

There was something mysterious about my granny, something she was hiding. I felt it in my bones. I was eleven and loved Nancy Drew, loved to investigate. I often hid under the big four-poster bed or in the dark closet while Granny talked on the phone in the evening. Waiting. Thinking I would finally know the secret. But she talked about work and food prices.

Mother was in the deep iron claw-foot tub with the water filled to the very top. Granny would hate this if she knew. I sat on a stool beside Mother and watched her body when the bubbles separated and allowed me a glimpse. I never wanted to be a woman. I wished to always remain a girl.

"There were two daughters." Mother said this with her eyes closed.

Because it was summer, there was still light outside. A hard rain fell, and I watched it run down the small window panes. I didn't speak. Only listened. I had learned this got me more information.

"I was the older sister by two years. Her name was Jeneva Estell. I thought she was pretty. Your granny called her Estell but I loved the name Jeneva. You have a brother instead of a sister."

And he made me mad because he got all the attention. I didn't even like his name: Jeff.

"I can't talk about anything that happened. It's not my place. But I will say, one day she was just gone from our lives, and I never saw her again. Don't ever wish your brother gone, Ann. It might happen."

I'm ashamed to say I hoped this would be the case.

Two days went by and I stood in the kitchen with Granny. A black cloud had darkened the room even more than the pine paneling. It was Tuesday, Granny's off day.

"Mother said she had a sister and she disappeared. She said I shouldn't ever wish Jeff gone or he might disappear too."

Granny clicked her tongue and looked out at the black clouds bunched together, threatening to let go of rain at any minute. "Annie, you don't need a man. You never need a man in your life. You can get along without them." Her words were measured, weighted, like she had been waiting for this question since I was born. The problem was the answer she gave didn't fit. "Your grandfather started drinking bad after Estell died. She was a tiny thing. His heart broke. He loved her so much. He stopped drinking when your mama was born, made a promise to God if he let her live he wouldn't drink a drop and he didn't. When Estell came, she looked just like Lizzie, his mama. Life was good. Then she died. He started drinking the day we buried her. She was sixteen months old." Granny walked out of the kitchen, and I heard the back door rattle as she walked left the house.

Less than two years after Jeanette's Christmas birth, Jeneva Estell Lord was born on November 23, 1931. She came into the world early just like Jeanette, but this time the pregnancy was further along and the birth wasn't as dramatic. Estell weighed more, and Dr. Brooks did not suggest this baby be thrown away. With the birth of this perfect baby, who looked exactly like Lizzie, JD continued to uphold his promise of not drinking that he had made when Jeanette survived. He was actually joyous.

JD and Inas still lived on Burke Road in the community of Shallow Ford, located in the most northern point of Dekalb County close to the community of Dunwoody, some seven miles southwest of Ernest and Henry Lee. George Washington Lord, JD's uncle, was one of the founding fathers of Dunwoody in 1823 and settled in the Mount Vernon Road area. At the time, the Cherokee were still in possession of the land. JD could trace his paternal side back to John Lord, who was born in Virginia in 1707, so his family was well respected throughout the community they helped begin. People were known to turn their heads and pretend not to notice if one of the Lord boys chose to drink a little too much and cause some innocent trouble. JD loved his liquor like many of the men in the community. After all, it was the Depression. The truth was that JD had been drinking since he was a young boy.

By 1931, JD and Inas, twenty-three and twenty-one, were the youngest couple on Burke Road. The Lord household was the only family with a "radio set," as listed in the 1930 census. JD was a farmer, and Inas was a housewife and mother of a newborn and a toddler. She must have been friends with her neighbor Viola Collins, who was also twenty-two, married to William, who was fifty-three with five children, ages fifteen to six, from his first wife.

The Depression had dug in its heels for a nice long stay and became a way of life. Noonday dinner for JD was often a pot of pinto beans—with a little fatback if they were lucky—and a pan of cornbread. They would eat the same thing that night, and sometimes Inas would bring out the fresh milk from the milking cow. The two would crumble cornbread in glass canning jars, covering it with the milk. Jeanette, who was not quite three, would beg for cornbread and milk too. Inas always shared hers and never fussed about what food—or lack thereof—they had each day. Her good-sized vegetable garden behind the house made it possible to can green beans, squash, corn, and tomatoes. Her laying hens gave the family eggs and allowed her to trade the extras with other families for items she didn't have, such as fatback and occasionally bacon. The Burke Farm down the road had apple trees, and the couple allowed Inas to get as many as she wanted. These were dried in the sun and placed in canning jars so Inas could make her famous fried pies sprinkled with sugar. So many other folks were worse off than her little family. One morning, early during the Depression, two hobos came to her door. She fed them bowls of beans and biscuits left over from dinner the night before. She wrapped the extra biscuits in a tea cloth and sent them with the men, who thanked her and went on their way to the river within minutes of having eaten the food, but not before they left a mark on a tree to let others know a good soul lived in the house and would share food. Inas often defended her feeding of the desperate men, saying one day she might need a helping hand.

The Thanksgiving Estell was born, the small family had baked hen, green beans, cornbread dressing, and turnip greens seasoned with a large chunk of fatback. The feast was worth sacrificing one of Inas's laying hens. There was much to celebrate with the coming of the new baby girl.

Estell became the love of the family. She had white-blond hair and blue eyes and began walking two months before she turned one. Jeanette still wasn't walking but got around just the same by dragging herself with her arms. She even pulled up on the chair seats and stood for long periods at a time, looking like a completely normal toddler. But the child wouldn't or couldn't take a step. She too had white-blond hair and blue eyes, but her features were just like Inas's, and this made Inas a little softer toward Jeanette. Both JD and Inas must have worried over Jeanette's lack of ability, especially in a time when any physical defect was shunned and considered shameful, a punishment from God. The little family passed through the next year with enough food, wood, good crops, and a decent house. Life was good.

On March 29, 1933, sixteen-month-old Estell woke with a fever. By the afternoon it was very high. Inas never talked of taking Estell to the hospital, the nearest being St. Joesph in Atlanta, where Henry Lee had died.

Years later, Inas told me Estell's story while I visited her one afternoon with my almost two-year-old daughter, Cassey, Inas's great-granddaughter.

"She looks like Estell the way she smiles and how she watches you with those big eyes, taking in everything you say." Her voice became soft and sad. "I never knew how sick she was until she was almost dead. It happened so fast. The doctor insisted she couldn't be saved, even if I had I brought her in the minute she began to run the fever. I think he was being nice. He said not many people, especially young children, survived spinal meningitis. She died shortly after he told me this. It was hot that day like summer, almost eighty degrees. And my baby girl just stopped breathing."

Death in Inas's early life was a specter hanging in the shadows, but the death of her youngest daughter would forever shape the way she lived her life for better or worse.

Jeneva Estell Lord was buried on Friday, March 31, 1933—the day after her death—in Mt. Pisgah United Methodist Church Cemetery without a marker because Inas and JD didn't have the money. The gathering of family and friends stood in the warm sunny afternoon and watched as this child was lowered into the ground. Within an hour, the group broke and went back to their lives as usual. After the funeral, JD found some whisky.

Life would deteriorate quickly for Inas. Not long after Estell's death, JD, Inas, and Jeanette moved to a small house across the street from Ernest. This was one of the properties that Ernest had acquired because of the Depression. By this point, Ernest owned the large amount of acreage he would later sell in the 1970s, making him a millionaire. But to look at him and his lifestyle in later years, one would never guess his wealth.

Inas and JD could no longer pay the rent on their small farm on Burke Road. JD stopped planting. Ernest decided to bring his sister closer to keep an eye on her little family. This shows he cared deeply for Inas. And, as someone who helped sell the liquor that intoxicated most men in the area, he was well aware of JD's drinking habits and how they had appeared again after Estell's death. Ernest knew about JD's raging drunkenness—about threats to have him thrown in jail—even if Inas didn't want to admit to them. What wife would admit such a problem? The family of three moved into the home, and Inas worked hard to save their lives.

Stone 13
Give the Child Away

Fast-forward to early 2017. I am fifty-nine and writing this book. I go in search of the area where Granny took me when I was ten, the old homeplace. The roads are altered. Holcomb Bridge is now a five-lane, congested highway, but Fouts Road is still there. The homeplace has been sold, torn down. I am pleasantly surprised with what I find. There is now a large park with lots of open fields and woods with long walking paths. This enables me to walk the land that my family came to own in 1919—my history, legacy, the last place Inas and JD would live together. Ironically, there is a large arts center on the land that holds classes and art shows. I walk the area that Inas and Bertha walked as children. I stand very still in the woods near a small creek and listen. The wind blows and I imagine all the stories of my grandparents blowing through me and scattering across the marsh and river. Somewhere they are watching this granddaughter. I pick up a stone from the path on this warm February day and hold it close to my heart. The Cherokee have a belief that rocks absorb energy like living things. This piece of my family's home sits on my desk along with a stone I took from Inas and Jeanette's graves. These stones are reminders of how heavy the past sits on the shoulders of the future.

JD now lived in a house that his outspoken brother-in-law owned. He was frowned on for not stepping up when his daughter died and taking care of his family, being a man. Most of the men in that area drank and occasionally got drunk, going home and taking it out on their loved ones, but they always took care of their families. JD broke the promises he made to God and Inas never to drink again. And Ernest was watching the details play out. The descriptions I've received of a young Ernest picture him as a no-nonsense businessman who would not have tolerated what he saw as a "weak" drunk. Inas must have attempted to cover for JD's work around the farm. The typical sharecropper's deal involved the owner providing the tools, land, and house. In return, the sharecropping family provided the owner with half of the cotton crop's proceeds or any crop proceeds. The family was allowed a small garden for their own food, but in some cases the owner would want a share of the vegetables, eggs, and meat the sharecropper managed to produce. Anything left after the family's needs were met was often traded at the local store for dried beans, flour, sugar, and cornmeal. Did Ernest expected his cut from JD and Inas? According to Inas, he did.

One evening in late spring after the family was settled in, JD came home drunk. What happened next I can only imagine because Granny never spoke of the scene. I was told of the incident by two of Ernest's daughters. Inas must have been tired, sad, and depressed, near her wit's end. Maybe she confronted JD when he came in the door reeking of liquor. The weight of their daughter's death sat squarely on both of their shoulders, making matters much worse. Or maybe he came home that night, took one look at his wife, and saw his sorrow strangling her. Maybe Inas threatened to leave, to tell her brother. Every male and female have a breaking point. JD broke in half that night. This is not to condone what he did; it is only an effort to understand the emotions driving his actions. How can someone physically and mentally beat the person they love most? Yet it happens all the time and could be commonplace in the thirties. That night, JD beat Inas with a rage that should have killed her. Where was Jeanette? I have to believe my mother witnessed the terrible assault. The house was tiny with one bed in the living room.

Ernest was standing on the porch of his house when Inas walked across the road holding Jeanette's hand. It was his niece's presence that helped him understand that the woman beside her was his little sister. Her eyes were nearly swollen shut and blood was everywhere. When Inas got close enough, Ernest erupted and called his brothers-in-law, Paul and Marcus Fouts, who lived close enough to hear him yell. The men set out to find JD, and within the hour they came dragging him into Ernest's backyard. JD was strung up between two trees with leather straps and beaten by the men. Their intent was to kill him.

"Stop." Ernest's wife Corine was a small woman but braver than most. "If you kill him, you will all go to prison. How will I take care of the children alone? He's not worth that."

Her brothers and husband stopped, cut down JD, and threw him in the back of a truck. Ernest drove until he got to Atlanta's city limits, where he forced the now sobering JD out of the truck.

"If you ever come back, we'll kill you." Ernest got back into the truck and drove away, leaving JD to find help.

JD did not come back to the Newtown area again, even though most of his family lived there. If he did, Ernest never found out about it.

Now, Inas was without a way to support herself and Jeanette. Her father was dead, not that he would have helped her, and her in-laws had passed too. Inas was twenty-four years old. A decision had to be made. Where would she and her daughter live? Then her older sister Beatrice made a visit to Ernest's house.

Inas's relationship with Beatrice always confused me. She wore a sour expression when she was around Inas and her family, as if she was among the most distasteful people instead of relatives. She dressed perfectly in Chanel suits and wore her salt-and-pepper hair in tight pin curls that hugged her scalp. Only once did I visit her house close to Atlanta: a long, sprawling, spotless brick ranch full of stiff, lifeless furnishings, the kind of decor you imagine being wrapped in plastic so it cannot get soiled. No family photos hung down the hall or sat on the end tables. The whole room reminded me of a furniture store. Throughout our visit, I imagined I was a mannequin in Rich's Department Store, where Inas worked. I understood the importance of being good for Inas so that Aunt Beatrice would be impressed. The two women talked as if they were on one of their nightly phone calls, devoid of emotion, not even a piece of gossip. I often wondered if this was what it was like to have a sister. After I was grown, Granny told me the story of what happened when Beatrice came to see her at Ernest's house after JD had been banished.

Beatrice married William Edward Bradley on December 23, 1925, in Aiken, South Carolina. By 1933 William was well on his way to being a financially successful businessman. The couple lived in a beautiful home on Hartford Avenue almost in the heart of Atlanta. William worked as a foreman at the power company. Beatrice and Inas were pregnant at the same time, Inas with Estell and Beatrice with her first, Harold Edward Bradley. Did the sisters talk at this time? Had Inas given her big sister advice on being pregnant? The two were more alike than they knew. Both looked alike and smiled the same way. But as similar as they were, Beatrice and Inas had very different lives. This must have caused some kind of divide between them.

When Beatrice came to visit Inas in late spring after JD had been run off, her young son in tow, she found her younger sister badly beaten. She was dressed for the occasion; that is something the two had in common—a love of dressing up. Being Beatrice, she attempted to act like Inas was not bruised and battered. But she must have ached for the girl she helped to raise. And there is a chance that she had developed pity for her family left back in Newtown. Beatrice had a plan for Inas: Inas would give up Jeanette to one of the orphan's homes that were so popular during the Depression. Beatrice would not have her handicapped niece living in her house. Then, once Jeanette was tossed aside, Inas could come work for Beatrice, caring for Harold, her young son, and keeping house. This is the second time the suggestion was made to throw Jeanette away. I can't help but wonder how these stories wore on my mother's self-esteem.

Inas refused Beatrice on the spot. Corine backed her up, explaining that Inas and Jeanette would live with her and Ernest as long as they needed. With this offer, Corine and Inas became closer than ever. Staying with her brother Ernest was not Inas's first choice, but the arrangement allowed her to keep her child. On that day, Inas was more determined than ever that Jeanette would walk.

From that day forward, Inas always held Beatrice at arm's length. She wore a fake smile and kept her business hidden from this woman who happened to be her sister by blood only. But at the same time, the way Beatrice treated Inas became Inas's inspiration to amount to something much better, no matter what she had to do to gain that kind of life. She would always measure her life against bossy Beatrice's and make decisions to help her achieve her goal.

Stone 14
The Widow

One photo remains of Inas after JD left Newtown. She is twenty-four, thin, with mournful eyes. Her hair is still short, but she no longer looks like a woman stepping out of the roaring twenties. The year is 1934, and she stands with Corine and her three daughters, who wear big smiles on their faces. In front of Inas is my mother, Jeanette. This is the only known photo of Jeanette as a small child. Her face is turned away with a determined brooding expression. So much about this photo reminds me of my childhood pictures; so much about the turn of her head and the wispy blond hair reminds me that I am her daughter, no mistaking the resemblance. Jeanette is wearing a light-colored sleeveless dress, while Corine's girls wear stylish jumper pant suits. I'd be willing bet that Inas sewed her daughter's dress. She was a master at creating beautiful clothing that looked store-bought. Unlike Jeanette, Inas is staring straight into the camera with a slight smile on her lips. Most would think she isn't smiling, but I know my grandmother's expressions. Her full smiles and hearty laughs were rare indeed. The whole group reminds me of a Dorothea Lange portrait.* When I compare this image of Inas with the family portrait of Asalee and Henry Lee, I see a mixture of both parents in Inas's face. She has Asalee's straight and narrow nose but Henry Lee's chin

---

* Dorothea Lange was famous for the photos she took of displaced farmers during the Great Depression. "Migrant Mother" was her iconic image. See "Dorothea Lange Biography," *Biography*, April 12, 2019, www.biography.com/artist/dorothea-lange.

and cheekbones. And there is a cockiness in her look that came from Henry Lee. One thing is for certain: Inas holds herself like Asalee, as if to ward off the next blow. She is fighting to recover her losses, trying to stay strong for her remaining child.

Jacob D. Lord is my grandfather, and until I set out to find him, I knew next to nothing about him. Even now, I don't know the color of his hair or eyes. Jeanette always believed his name was Joseph Dean. Inas never corrected her, or maybe she is the one who told her this untruth. How can a daughter live with her father until she is five and not learn his name? This man did not abandon her but was rightly sent away. Why would a mother not tell her child the name of her father? Too many questions. Inas kept many secrets close to her that were not shared with Jeanette. The two never sat down and discussed the beating Inas took that night from JD. Inas pretended the incident never happened, which was surely very confusing for a child. Jeanette witnessed violent behavior from her father. This had to leave a scar. A discussion was due. One day JD was there, and the next he was gone just like when Estell died. Jeanette must have believed he had died too.

In my early twenties, when I visited Granny at her house, she brought up the subject of JD for the second and last time in my life. "Your grandfather went back to drinking and left me with your mother. He went to South Georgia and lived near the Okefenokee Swamp, where he caught malaria from mosquito bites. He ended up in Grady Hospital in Atlanta. I went and sat with him. I was there the day he died. Annie, I've seen three people die in my lifetime: my mother-in-law, my baby girl, and your grandfather. That is enough for me." She stood up then. "Let's go make some lunch. Enough sad talk." And that was it. She offered no more information.

JD's last known address was not actually the Okefenokee Swamp. He spent his last months of life at 294 Pryor Street in downtown Atlanta. If he worked, I could not find any records. While JD lived in Atlanta, Inas was busy at Ernest's house. She and Corine became like sisters. Jeanette finally began walking, but with a lopsided hobble that would remain with her to some degree for the rest of her life. Jeanette was beautiful and loved playing with Audrey, Corine and Ernest's third child, who was the same age as Jeanette.

Inas helped with the family garden, cooking, sewing, and putting food up for winter. One of the hot summer afternoons, while Corine and Inas worked in the kitchen, Jeanette and Audrey went out to the barn. Permanent waves for women's hair was all the rage at the time, and like any little girls, Audrey and Jeanette loved to play that they were grown women. This day, they planned to play beauty shop. The two went to where the tractor was parked. Audrey rummaged around the tools until she found what she wanted, axle grease—perfect for the gook used to roll up women's hair to make waves and curls. Audrey sat Jeanette down on a wooden milking stool and combed her wispy blond hair. She slathered the axle grease onto the strands until Jeanette's whole head of hair was shiny black.

When Inas found the girls, she let out a scream that made Jeanette cry.

No matter how many times my mother told this story, Granny never laughed. She didn't even crack a smile.

First, Inas attempted to wash Jeanette's hair with hot water. The grease only repelled the water that beaded all over her head. Then Corine had the idea to try petroleum jelly, Ernest used to clean his greasy hands. The jelly was smeared and combed through Jeanette's greasy hair. Rags were used to wipe the grease out. Slowly, the stuff broke down and was removed. Several washings later, dark patches marked Jeanette's light hair. More than two weeks of washing passed before Jeanette's hair was back to normal. Not long after this, her hair began to curl. By the time she was eight, it was so curly and thick that it was hard to get a comb through it.

Inas began working at a local "tavern," "speakeasy," or "juke joint"—a socially questionable establishment of the times—waiting tables to make her own money. She wanted to leave Ernest's house, but he ordered her to quit working there. She quit the job and started working for a woman, keeping her child and cleaning house. Once again, Ernest got in the way; he held the mortgage on this woman's farm and threatened to call her loan if she didn't fire Inas. Why would Ernest act like this? Inas claimed he was controlling and didn't want his sister to live on her own. He felt she had made too many bad decisions and needed to stay with him.

Sometime between June 22 and 27 of 1934, Inas received the news that JD was gravely ill in the hospital. I imagine she asked Corine to watch Jeanette and went to JD. Who would have driven her, since she had no car? However Inas got there, she stayed until JD died.

When I found JD's death certificate, I noted many discrepancies in Inas's story of how he died. He was admitted to Butler Hall, the original name for Grady Hospital, on June 22, Inas's twenty-fifth birthday. In contrast to what Granny had told me, JD did not die of malaria. His doctor was L. Minor Blackford, a well-known and respected doctor in Atlanta who was also affiliated with Emory Hospital. JD's diagnosis was intestinal obstruction due to scarring caused by an old appendectomy. Cachexia had set in. This disorder causes extreme weight and muscle loss, and eating will not reverse the damage.

JD's death didn't resemble Inas's story. Was she really there with him? Did she speak to the doctor? Inas did bring his body back to be buried by their youngest child, little Estell. JD too went without a headstone until much later, and by then Inas was living one of the biggest lies a woman could live. This untruth was huge, so all-encompassing that she changed the last name of her husband and children. The headstones of JD and Estell read Loyd rather than Lord. By the time I came along, Mother used Loyd as her maiden name.

Inas was a widow, and her life was about to take a turn from hard to harder. But Inas was so determined to have her way that she didn't care how tough her life would become.

Stone 15
Urban Legend

I am nineteen and the year is 1976. I am married and have my first daughter, Melissa. Every day I visit Granny, who is alone now with a lot of time on her hands since she retired from Rich's Department Store after thirty-eight years, and since her devoted brother, Arthur, my great-uncle who visited her several times a week, died of a heart attack at her house in 1971.

Each day Granny and I have long conversations that I crave. It is spring, and the warm air sifts through the open window above the sofa in the living room. The furniture in the house sits exactly where it did when I came to live there as a child. I take comfort in the familiar settings that nurture me. I can still count on some things to stay the same. Outside the window, the sun dots the driveway, and the dancing leaf shadows catch my attention, reminding me of the afternoons I spent telling stories to myself as I walked up and down the driveway. Being in this room with Granny feels safe. I am accepted. She begins to speak. The story for this afternoon weaves an urban legend that I will carry thirty years into the future before I finally explode the myth.

Right now, as she tells it, I believe.

Sometime before or just after JD's death, Jeanette began to have horrible throat infections. Inas decided enough was enough. She would not watch another person close to her die if she could help stop it from happening. While antibiotics were still yet to be developed, there were new ways to treat throat infections or help prevent them. Dr. Brooks explained that Jeanette's tonsils could be removed, and this would help lower the number of throat infections she suffered. The surgical procedure, while not perfectly safe, was Inas's best choice. A week in the hospital and a sore throat treated with cold ice cream would help Jeanette recover quickly.

When Inas explained the option to Ernest and Corine, her brother thought it was overreacting to perform an expensive operation on a child who had a few sore throats. He viewed the loss of his younger sisters as tragic but unpreventable. He did not believe removing Jeanette's tonsils would keep her from getting serious throat infections. And he was correct. The removal of Jeanette's tonsils might minimize the frequency of strep, but she would likely still get the illness if exposed.

Inas would not accept Ernest's final word on this subject. She began to work for women, watching their children and doing their laundry. The same battle between brother and sister ensued. When Ernest got wind of a job, he would go to the employer and threaten them. He had a lot of pull in the community whether he owned the property or not. Inas always lost her job.

One day, Inas couldn't bear Ernest's control any longer. She placed her and Jeanette's belongings in a flour sack. Mother and daughter set out walking with no idea where to go. She only knew she couldn't stay around Newtown anymore.

The sun heated the dirt road under Jeanette's bare feet and she fretted, but Inas encouraged her to keep going. The dust stirred with each gust of wind, coating the trees, their feet, hair, and clothes. Inas wanted it to rain, thought about how wonderful the mud would feel. She had no food and no idea where to sleep. When the sun balanced on the treetops and began to sink from the sky, she thought about what was left behind: a decent bed, hot meals, and a roof over their heads. Not to mention her friendship with Corine. At sundown Inas took Jeanette to a barn that had seen better days, and they slept together in the hay. Mother and daughter watched the stars through the holes in the roof. The next morning Jeanette cried for food, having not eaten since the morning before. Inas, who also needed food, took Jeanette's hand and began walking again, not having a clue where she would go or what she would do. As Jeanette began to whimper, Inas thought about turning back, returning to Ernest and begging to live in his house, agreeing to forget the operation and his limitations on her work. Maybe she had to turn around for her child. And then a rumbling came from behind her. Dust billowed above the hill that they had walked down minutes before. A dump truck topped the hill, and Inas pulled Jeanette into the ditch for safety.

Instead of passing Inas, the driver stopped in the middle of the road and stepped out.

"Why are you two ladies walking this road so early in the morning?"

Inas never told me her response, but the man was Arthur Owens, and he took mother and daughter to eat and then got them a room in a boarding house just off the square in Marietta, Georgia, some thirty miles southwest of Newtown. This act of kindness began a forty-year affair between Arthur and Inas. And no, he was not her brother.

So bewitched was I with this telling that, thirty years later,

I wrote the scene into my third novel *Where the Souls Go* and called the man "Cove."

The road Inas was traveling doesn't exist today, but when I was ten we traced the same route once or twice a month to visit her sisters. Mother never missed an opportunity to point out an old barn, black with age, that sat high on an embankment.

"You know you're poor when you sleep in a barn with hay for a bed and look at the stars through the cracks in the roof. Chickens ran around under the floor. Staying there made me so afraid of the dark."

Inas never responded on these trips; she always did the driving. She kept her eyes on the road with her mouth pinched like a bow, her expression screaming distaste. Her body language shouted traitor. Each time I made the trip—even after I was grown and the road was still there—I looked for the barn. A worry lodged itself in my mind when I was a child that I would be without a home too. If a woman like Inas could be homeless, surely I could lose my place to live. To this day, even after I know the bigger story, one of my greatest fears is being without a place to live.

Hearing Granny's story that spring afternoon in 1976, I was struck silent. Arthur, the man I had always believed was her brother, my great-uncle, had actually been her lover. The first time I met Arthur was shortly after my father left and we lived with Granny. Arthur came every Sunday night for dinner around 7:00 pm. He always brought two brown paper lunch bags of candy and four dollars in quarters, two for me and two for Jeff. This was a lot of money for children in 1968. Arthur never came for Thanksgiving, but he always showed up late on Christmas morning.

The first summer I lived with Inas, she took Jeff and me on a picnic to meet Arthur at a burned-out house that sat off the road on a lot of land. Inas and Arthur sat in folding lawn chairs as Jeff and I ran through the charred ruins of the house—probably not the safest place for us to play but a kid's delight all the same. I was in my Nancy Drew phase and saw the house as a mystery to be solved. Secrets lurked in every corner. And, I wouldn't know for many years how right I was about the existence of those secrets.

Jeff and I were deep into play that hot summer afternoon when I saw Arthur counting several one-hundred-dollar bills into Inas's hand. There were at least ten bills, a fortune in 1968.

"Wow," I yelled. I'd never seen a bill bigger than twenty.

Inas frowned and told me I was acting rude and ignorant. I wonder if I detected a hint of embarrassment or shame. It was the unspoken Southern rule not to speak of money. I guess I was supposed to act like I had seen one-hundred-dollar bills all my short life.

Every part of me believed the story Inas told me in 1976, believed she wasn't ashamed for making the choice to let Arthur help her so many years before. Her choices were limited as a woman and the sister of Ernest Hawkins. She had tried to live her life the right way on her own. She also explained that feeling shame for her love was futile. This man became her heart and soul. Their relationship lasted much longer than a lot of marriages. Arthur did right by his own wife and kids, and he was also there for Inas and Jeanette. She ended the story with a question.

"What would have happened had Arthur not come along in his dump truck that day?"

The thought made me shudder. In that question, I saw

Inas as a hero, a strong woman determined to save her remaining child. Her husband had died and left her with a brother she had come to think of as mean and controlling. What else could she do?

Inas never mentioned whether Jeanette had the operation to remove her tonsils. She spun this tale like Rapunzel spun wheat into gold in the old fairytale. I am still filled with pride knowing that Granny did what she had to do to save my mother. But as it turns out, that wasn't the real story at all.

Stone 16
The History of a Lover

Arthur A. Owens was born January 1, 1903, a New Year baby, to twenty-four-year-old Oscar Owens and twenty-year-old Ida Bell Hawkins Owens in Gordon County, Georgia. Arthur was the second child and first son of the couple. Oscar's parents, John and Eliza Owens, and Ida's parents, Claiborn and Georgia Hawkins, lived close by with their own large families. Both sets of parents had children ranging from seventeen to newborn still living at home.

Claiborn and Georgia were transplants from the Hightower Community in Forsyth County some sixty miles southeast. When they moved their family in 1899, the couple left behind two of their grown children. Henry Lee and Asalee were among those who remained in Hightower. Ida Bell was Henry Lee's younger sister by five years. This made Arthur Henry Lee's nephew and Inas's first cousin.

In 1910 when Inas was one year old, seven-year-old Arthur lived in Dalton, Georgia. One has to wonder when Inas first came in contact with him. Did Ida Bell bring her family back to Hightower for Asalee's funeral? Was this the first time Inas met her first cousin, or was it earlier when Aunt Ida Bell came for a visit? How well did Inas know Arthur as a child? As much as I would like to say Inas didn't know Arthur was her first cousin when they met as adults, I find this nearly impossible to believe.

By 1920, Oscar and Ida Bell had moved their family to Macon, Georgia. Oscar was a farm laborer on a fruit farm, probably one of the many peach orchards that are still plentiful today. Arthur was sixteen and began courting Mattie Fretwell, who was also sixteen. Mattie lived with her twenty-three-year-old brother, Jasper, and four other siblings. Jasper was the head of the house. While their parents, JT, forty-four, and Mary, thirty-five, are shown living with the family in 1910, their names disappear by 1920. This suggests that Mattie's parents had died. The Spanish flu killed many in the years of 1917–1919. This seems to be a plausible reason for Jasper to be caring for the family.

On December 25, 1920, Arthur and Mattie were married. Their first child, Arthur A. Owens Jr., was born on October 1, 1922. Inas was a mere child of twelve in 1922, recovering from the death of Bertha. Jerry Owens, the couple's second son, was born in 1927. Arthur moved his family to Madison, Tennessee, in 1930 and worked for W. Y. Williams of the State Highway Department. This was a good job for the beginning of the Great Depression, and it corroborates Inas's story that Arthur drove a dump truck for the highway department in 1934. Between 1930 and 1934, Arthur was doing so well that he moved Mattie and his two sons to Powder Springs, Georgia, in Cobb County, where he bought a house for $1,500.00.

Part of Inas's story of being rescued by Arthur was that he took her to a boarding house in Marietta and rented mother and daughter a room off the Marietta Square on Waterman Street. Inas and Jeanette didn't stay in the boarding house long because Arthur got a long-term project in Cuthbert, Georgia, located just below Columbus, and he took Inas and Jeanette there to live with him.

Mattie may have known of Inas as Arthur's first cousin, but at this point, I think it is safe to guess she was not aware

Inas was Arthur's mistress.

In a letter shortly after Jeanette's death, the information that Arthur and Inas were first cousins was shared with me by Audrey Lee, Ernest and Corine's third child and Jeanette's first cousin and childhood friend. "So now you understand why my daddy Ernest couldn't have her living with our family. He warned her several times and Inas wouldn't listen. She continued to see their first cousin and that ended things."

These words radically changed the story Inas had told me in 1976. She did not become homeless because Ernest was mean and didn't want Jeanette to have an operation. She was told to leave because she was having an affair with Arthur, something that was completely unacceptable even if he hadn't been a first cousin. I have a watery childhood memory of Inas telling me she had spent time at a building taken over by squatters, people with no jobs, near the river close to Roswell, Georgia. Was this a cardboard jungle? Why was she there? I'm not sure. Did she stay there before she found the barn? Had she been making her way to Arthur all along? I have to question whether Arthur ever picked up Inas and Jeanette off the side of the road. Maybe this was Inas's fictional story that she told so much she began to believe it as truth.

While Arthur was a large part of my childhood, there are no photos of him—only photos of his car with Audrey in front of it. Inas left with Arthur in 1934 after JD's death. They remained in a relationship until 1971, thirty-seven years.

Stone 17
Debunking a Myth

Imagine being only five years old and fending for yourself in one room, in a boarding house where you don't know anyone, in a city you've never visited. This is the story Mother told Jeff and me as kids. Inas left her only child alone in the middle of a bed with orders not to get up. To keep her occupied, there was a pair of scissors and a Sears and Roebuck catalog. Jeanette entertained herself by cutting out people from the pages, along with clothes. She created a self-made paper doll family to replace the one she had lost.

The year JD died was a dark time for Jeanette. When Inas left Ernest's house, she altered not only her life but the life of her young daughter, who lost her best friend Audrey, her aunt and uncle, and the home she had known. Years would go by before Jeanette would rekindle a friendship with Audrey.

When I began researching the years of 1935–1940, I came up empty when trying to place Inas. I searched for the boarding house on Waterman Street in Marietta. I decided to look outside the borders of the state and was on the trail again. Jeanette's story of being alone for long hours in the boarding house may have been true, but the length of time mother and daughter stayed there was short.

In the census dated April 5, 1940, a new category was added: Inferred Residence in 1935. Inas, Jeanette, and Arthur were living in Cuthburt, Georgia, just below Columbus. In 1940 the three are listed as living in Lancaster, South Carolina, at 210 Arch Street West. Arthur is the head the household. Inas is stated to be his wife, with a line drawn through the word and "cousin" written instead. Arthur is now a superintendent and reports an annual income as $2,460.00, a nice sum for this time period. Jeanette is ten. Inas is noted as married, not a widow. Both Jeanette and Inas's last name has changed from Lord to Loyd. In the 1930 census, by contrast, JD, Inas, and Jeanette have their last name as Lord.

Until I found the 1940 census, I held out hope that Audrey had made a terrible mistake about Inas and Arthur being first cousins and about Inas changing her name. But the proof was in the official historical document. JD was erased not only from Jeanette's life but also from her memory. She became a Loyd with a father who wasn't dead a year before her mother was with another man. How might this have affected Jeanette's mental illness later in her life? In one of her low points, Mother once said, "Your grandmother isn't who you think she is, Ann." She spoke with such venom it frightened me. I worried she might be telling the truth.

I could guess the name change was Inas and Arthur's way of hiding Inas's identity from Mattie. Surely Arthur still being married to Mattie was a sign to Inas that he would never leave his wife for her. Was it love that kept Inas with Arthur? Or was it the need of income, a way to live and to raise her child? Whatever her reasons, Inas had been with Arthur a little over five years at this point. I have to wonder if Mattie was still in the dark.

On May 9, 1940, Arthur A. Owens appears on a second census record, a month and four days since he took the census in South Carolina. Now he is listed as living in Powder Springs, Georgia, with Mattie. His annual income has dropped to $1,525.00. Was this Arthur's attempt to hide his second family by reporting lower wages? His expenses in Lancaster must have been around $950.00 a year.

Mattie lived in a small house with their two sons. Did she begin to question Arthur because he was gone all the time? Or was she proud that he provided a good living when so many were barely scraping by? Arthur must have shined like a hero in Mattie's mind.

I found myself pondering Mattie's situation. I wanted to understand what she was like, what her life was like with Arthur only home on an occasional weekend. She must have had a big garden with two sons to help tend it. Maybe they had a field of corn for selling as livestock feed. In all likelihood, she had laying hens, maybe a cow. Mattie couldn't have been a whiny, clinging wife. She ran her place alone. She did more than manage. She made a life.

This is the part of the urban legend that turns sour: two women financially dependent on one man. To judge either one of them by today's standards is futile. Their circumstances were much different in 1940 than a woman's would be today. Mattie and her sons were clearly the victims of bad choices made by Inas and Arthur. The repercussions for Jeanette are still unfathomable. Arthur is to blame in many ways for what he did to his boys and wife. At some point he should have stopped playing games, having his cake and eating it too, and made a clean break, walked away from Inas or Mattie. He had a choice. And why did Inas remain with Arthur almost forty years, long after the time when she stood on her own two feet financially and emotionally? Did she ever feel bad for what Mattie and her sons went through when they discovered the affair? Most of all, how did these choices affect Jeanette? The scandalous relationship caused Inas to be shunned, similar to

Henry Lee, by her family and community. History repeated itself.

Part Five

Ann

Stone 18
An Orphan's Journal

Spring 2003

I insist on living in natural light-filled spaces. I crave the outdoors, open land, and long walks in the woods near some kind of running water and huge oak trees. It is no accident I live within four miles of a national park. This is the life that feeds my creativity and allows my imagination to run wild. I am sure I was adopted or dropped by aliens into my family.

Granny had only one use for outside: work. She loved a flower garden better than anyone. There was always something blooming: four o'clocks, jonquils, zinnias, and hydrangeas. She would suit up in a long-sleeve buttoned-up blouse, long thick pants, sturdy shoes, and a large floppy straw hat. No matter how hot it was, Granny wore this uniform. Many times I dropped by for a visit and found her mowing the grass with a push mower. Her face was beet red, and sweat rolled down from the top of her head into her eyes. In her seventies, several moles came up on her nose. She went to the doctor and was diagnosed with skin cancer. The doctor believed this was due to her long exposure to the sun when working in the cotton fields as a child. This did not stop her from having her flowers.

Granny took great pleasure and pride in her plants and yard. Whenever I visited—which was often—she gave me a small envelope of seeds that she had gathered for me. Often I would come home with bush cuttings too. My love for growing things came from her. But Granny never sat out in the backyard and enjoyed her work. No cookouts, no watching the kids play in a wading pool, no stargazing. She had little use for the outdoors in a casual sense. She had little use for fun.

Mother never goes outside for anything except getting in her car to go shopping, her favorite pastime. I often wonder how my brother learned to ride a bike so well. Or how I learned to play basketball and swim. I recall two times when Mother was outside with the intention of being there. Once when I was ten, we went to the local lake beach with her best friend, Polly, and her daughters. Polly was a handsome, six-foot-tall woman, athletic and brave. Polly and Mother were complete opposites. Polly and her daughters swam out to the diving platform in the deep water while Mother, Jeff, and I remained in the shallow water no deeper than my waist. Mother's very pale skin turned pinker and pinker. By the time we reached Granny's house that evening, Mother's whole body was flaming red and so were Jeff's and mine. This was before the use of sunblock. Granny made a clicking sound with her tongue when she saw us. She didn't have to say anything. We already knew how she felt.

That night Mother spread cold cream on my shoulders and back. For a full minute, I thought my burning skin had been healed, but the tingling moved from somewhere deep under the sunburn, building with intensity until my shoulders and face were on fire once again. Never again would Mother go into the water. Instead, on a vacation trip to Florida the following year, she sat in the open door of our hotel room and tried to watch us in the surf far away from the door. Had we been in danger, she couldn't have made it across the beach to us in a timely manner due to the weight she had put on and her handicap; even then, had she reached us, she couldn't swim. Granny had never allowed her to learn to swim or play in the water.

Mother sits at her sewing machine for hours at a time making heavy lined drapes to hang on all the windows to block out natural light and keep others—people who might want to hurt her—from seeing inside. Her home is a cave-like dwelling. A typical weekend finds her in bed, wearing a sexy, lacy nightgown, watching old movies all day and night unless she needs to go to the store.

Last summer I decided to invite her on a trip to St. Simons Island, one of Georgia's barrier islands. To my shock, she accepted and offered to drive. I agreed, wondering what the catch was. There was always a catch. I worried about how she would act on the trip. Her mental illness flared over the slightest disagreements or imagined offenses. On the first day, I took her to the lighthouse. The tide was high and the waves were crashing onto the grass and rocks close to where we were sitting in a gazebo. The lighthouse towered over us.

"Ann, this is beautiful. Thank you for bringing me." She patted my hand.

This is the only time I can remember Mother thanking me for anything, and one of the only times we enjoyed peace between each other as adults. As I watched her staring at the sea, I experienced a childlike wonder. This was the person I loved with the purest of love, a child's love. Yet she was a confusing contradiction. I touched her arm. "I'm glad you feel what I feel when I'm here."

She removed her arm from my touch. "Of course I do. I'm your mother. You get this love of the ocean from me. There is so much you don't know about me, Ann. But that is a good thing."

There is much more to this woman than the pills she takes to manage the wild voices in her head, the moods shifting out of control. Inside is a person with love she would like to share, but she doesn't know how. That day at the lighthouse was not the first time I thought Mother is really another woman, one filled with pain and fear that can't be managed.

Late Summer 2003

My fiction takes a sharp turn toward telling Granny's stories. This upcoming October will mark ten years since her death, and on many days it feels like only a small amount of time has passed. Somehow I unconsciously give myself permission to tell a story the way I want to tell it rather than thinking about what Granny would say. I write a story of a woman who chooses to stay with a married man named Arthur P. Sawyer and how this destroys her daughter, Jeanette.

I don't see Mother after my therapist tells me to give myself permission to stay away. So now I am free. Yes, free. I no longer have to anticipate Mother's next move, whether I can stop her from killing herself. Her sharp tongue can't slice me to ribbons any longer. The anticipation of the next shoe falling has dissipated into only thoughts of her. Sometimes vivid memories. Yet on some days I'm not free of her, and I don't want to be. Once I stepped away, she took the services the state offered. The first time she refused to go for her dialysis, the social worker assigned to her case suggested she go into assisted living. Mother agreed. Now she has a good diet and is forced to take care of herself. The fallout of course is that she wants nothing to do with me. I am a traitor. I abandoned her. And the truth is I did. I accept that I may not know if something happens to her. This is the price I will pay for her disapproval. This is the price I will pay for walking away. I own a strange peace with this choice.

September 27, 2003

It is Saturday, and the air is heavy with rain, but on most days this is a tease. We are living through one of the worst droughts Georgia has seen in years. The lawn is dry and crackles when I walk across it to get to the car. A weight sits on my shoulders and chest this morning. Mother creeps into my thoughts. To combat the feeling of loss, I go to a local walking trail. The gray clouds are low, and the air is thick. As I take the path down into this small valley near the large creek, my shoulders and face relax. I'm not clinching my teeth. A wet breeze blows over me, and the tension building for days is released. I walk the path by the winding creek. Early yellow fall leaves spin in the current. The sound of flowing water soothes me like a hot bath. A haunted melody floats from one of the houses high on the ridge and kisses me right in the chest. Music has always moved me. The haunting song is one that makes me think of lost love, the kind I'm glad didn't work out but ached for just the same. Mother was instrumental in breaking up one such relationship. At the time, I hated her for doing this. I was deeply in love. Of course I couldn't see her fight to separate me from this boy as an act of love. Now I know it was a deep love. There is love between us. The thought is a surprise. Sometimes the emotion is hard to find in reference to us, mother and daughter. The song plays over and over, and I can't help but think maybe it's just in my head. No one would play this same tune over and over again. But that's not true. I do this when I'm writing. Music helps me with experiencing my characters' emotions. The wind picks up and a rumble of thunder shakes the ground under my feet. The melody follows me until I begin the climb up the path and out of the valley. The beauty of the song and the memories it evokes stay behind. The sky opens as I get into the car. The long-awaited, prayed-for rain pounds my car, blurring the windows. There is no leaving. The road has disappeared into an abyss of gray water. Flashes of light turn pinkish outside my safe place. Thunder rolls for what seems like forever. Complete relaxation, relief, moves over me. For the first time since Mother began to take dialysis, I crumble into my feelings; my heart opens and I cry. I cry for all the days we haven't had. The times lost because of her mental illness or my fear of her mental illness. I cry, a child without her mother. But she loves me. It's right there in my heart, the love she couldn't hand me. Somehow this pure emotion has invaded me. I sob. After thirty minutes, the rain stops as abruptly as it began. The road home is right in front of me where it was all along. I put the window down. Fresh, cool air hits me in the face. The steamy heat has evaporated. I start the engine and go home.

Jeanette Lord Swafford died around the time the rain broke loose and our area began recovering from the long summer drought. She was seventy-four years old. She died alone in the hospital as I walked the trail and heard the music. Granny would say she reached out to me. I think this is true. She had been heading down a self-destructive road for more years than not. Her death leaves me hollow, off balance, raw, and alone. I am an orphan. The women who raised me have gone.

September 30, 2003

In the lobby after Mother's funeral, two elegant women around her age stand near a small sofa, watching me. One of the women has gray hair with a chic cut. When she walks, the dress coat she wears flips open to reveal a gray business suit. Her smile sparkles when she turns it on me.

"Are you, Ann, Jeanette's daughter?"

"Yes. I am." I can't even imagine Mother knowing anyone like this woman.

The other woman with dark, tightly curled hair—a little more old-fashioned—comes to stand beside us.

The chic woman speaks. "I am Audrey, and this is my sister Doris. Our father was Ernest Hawkins, Aunt Inas's older brother. We were your mother's first cousins, and I was her best friend until we were nineteen and I married."

"It's so nice to meet you." I take her soft hand in mine.

"I'm so sorry about Jeanette," Doris says. "We were all playmates when we were younger." She touches my arm.

So these women are my second cousins. I can't help but wonder how my idea of Granny's family would be different had I met them earlier. What truths would have been revealed?

"Do you remember our father?" Audrey asks.

"Yes. I met him a couple of times. I loved your mother. She was kind and soft-spoken." I wouldn't dare share that Granny told me Ernest was mean to Mother and her, not to mention his own children and wife. He threw Granny out of the house for wanting to get Mother's tonsils taken out, making them homeless during the Depression. Yet Granny always packed us in the car for our monthly trip to visit her sisters, Stella and Corine. Uncle Ernest was never around.

"We saw Jeff, but he didn't have much to say. I'm sure he was upset. We missed you when the family met for prayer."

I swallow my broken heart and a mean, edgy laugh. "To be honest, it's best I'm not around my brother. I know nothing about his life these days." This isn't exactly true, but Granny always said not to air our dirty laundry.

The night Mother died, I went to Jeff's house to tell him of her death in person. I called and let his wife Carla know I was making the trip. When I arrived, the windows were dark and no one came to the door. They had left rather than stay to see me. While I stood on his front porch, he was busting in the side window of Mother's house so he could replace the locks and keep me out. And as crazy as it might sound, Mother had probably left the request with him.

"We haven't talked in four years," I tell the sisters.

Doris looks away, but Audrey gives me a sad smile. "Doris's brother-in-law owns this funeral home. This has been where most of the Hawkins family had their funerals, at least three generations."

The image of Granny as part of a much larger family, as having traditions, jars me. She always stood within arm's distance of the sisters and cousins we visited.

"Your great-grandfather was here," Audrey continues. "My daddy and mama. I'm glad Inas and Jeanette were here too."

"Yes, it is time for them to really come home," Doris agrees. "Your mama was beautiful when she was young. All the boys wanted to date her."

This is a new story for me. To hear Mother talk, Dad had been her only boyfriend. "I've never seen photos of her when she was young. Only one of the night before she married my dad, and she was twenty-four by then."

Audrey pulls out a pen and paper from her purse. "Give me your address. We will send you photos. Every daughter should see her mother as child."

I write down my address.

"You know, Jeanette left me a message on my voicemail right before she died." Audrey arches her eyebrow at me, and her expression tells me the message must have indicated Mother's mental illness. By this point in her life, she could barely contain it. "She needed money. She seemed pretty desperate."

"Mother had a lot of problems before she died." What a bland response. How can I tell these elegant women how Mother finally lost her grip? How she wanted to die so badly she skipped her dialysis treatments for a week at a time? How she attached herself to Jack, my husband, but wanted nothing to do with me? How she had called my mother-in-law and begged for money? How Jack had found her unconscious on her bathroom floor and called 911? How my therapist had requested I take a break from Mother before she died and I blamed myself for her mental illness? How she died alone in a hospital, and the staff only called me out of desperation because my brother refused to answer his phone?

"Ann, your mother had problems when she was young too." Audrey's voice is soft. She takes my hand and pats it. There it is. I learn that Mother had battled mental illness since she was a young woman, and for one awful moment I am relieved.

"It was Aunt Inas who caused much of Jeanette's problems. The whole family knows this." Doris shakes her head, and Audrey gives her a warning look. "The girl should be told.

Did you know that Inas changed their last name when Jeanette was young? Your grandfather was a Lord. After his death, she changed her last name to Loyd and moved away."

My head roars. Had Mother known her name was changed? That she wasn't who she thought she was?

One Week after Mother's Death

A few days after the funeral, two large envelopes arrive in the mail. When I spill the contents on my bed, a young girl stares back at me. The photos reflect all different ages. I am looking in a mirror. Mother and I look like twins. Each time she gazed at me, she must have disliked what she saw. I reflected a younger her. I was doing all the things she had longed for, and I was succeeding.

That night I dream I am looking at an old sepia photo with ruffled edges. The young girl with long hair sits with her back to me and stares off at a ridge of mountains in the distance. Then she turns and looks at me—my mother, much younger.

"Don't tell your mother's story; tell mine."

I take a two-week leave of absence from my job as technical writer at BP Oil. In those two weeks, I write ten short stories. All of these pieces are accepted for publication within one month. I am to be a published writer, my longtime dream. Both Granny and Mother are gone. I have no one to answer to but myself. The dam has broken. The forbidden stories spill forth. But I still don't know the real truth of who these women are.

Part Six

Jeanette Loyd (Lord)

Stone 19
A Home of Their Own

Jeanette Mildred Lord, now Loyd, turned ten in the state of South Carolina, where she lived her mother's lie that would stretch far into her adulthood, altering her childhood stories and her identity, making her unsure of what memories were real and what were not. Often she spoke about visiting with her mother's friends in South Carolina. I never put two and two together to realize that she actually lived there.

Lancaster is an old city established in the mid-1700s by Scottish and English settlers, the Red Rose City, close to the metro area of North Carolina's Charlotte. In 1940, Arch Street was lined with moderately sized wooden framed homes. Jeanette had her own room and plenty of food. She attended school close to Arch Street, and it was here that children began to tease and bully her about the wobble in her walk. Also, she wasn't a good reader. Often Inas blamed this on Jeanette's premature birth, but I never saw proof that Mother struggled with reading. After all, this was the woman who read *Little Women* to me when I was three.

The years Jeanette lived in Lancaster are vague, a fuzzy view at best. Teachers at her school insisted on the best hygiene and graded the students on their appearance each morning. The children were inspected for tangles in their hair, dirty fingernails, skin cleanliness, and clean teeth, as if they were animals about to be sold. If one of the children had an infraction, he or she was hit several times on the palm with a wooden ruler. One sliver of dirt under a fingernail bought the child welts.

Jeanette lived in fear that she would miss something, and her aversion to dirt carried well into her adulthood. It didn't help, though, with her hoarding tendencies that came from the time she and her mother did without the things they needed.

Inas rarely made friends, so any visitors to the couple's house on Arch Street must have been Arthur's friends from work. Living in a house with Arthur was the closest Inas came to having a family with him. In a time when birth control was almost nonexistent, Inas had to work hard not to get pregnant again. One time when I was a teenager, she offered me the following valuable information: "Get birth control pills. Take them every day. When I was young, if a woman wanted to keep from having a baby, it was next to impossible. Her choices were not having relations with the man, using the rhythm system [calculating days from the end of one's period to find out ovulation time], and inserting a penny inside yourself to keep the man's seed from entering." At the time, I never imagined Inas was speaking about herself. One doesn't normally think of their grandmother in sexual terms. Her advice must have worked for her, because Inas never got pregnant with Arthur's child. Or if she did, the problem was taken care of without a record.

Earlier that year, in January 1940, the movie *Gone with the Wind* came out in theaters. Inas and Arthur took Jeanette to see it in Charlotte. This movie turned out to be one of Jeanette's favorites. She was captivated with Rhett Butler and vowed to find a man like him to marry. This movie caused her to turn her back on the Shirley Temple movies that she was obsessed with at an early age. Jeanette would always be a movie buff, watching classics like *Singin' in the Rain* over and over again. She was a diehard romantic to a fault. Seeing a film at the nearby theater cost only a nickel, and Arthur was generous with the nickels she requested. This love of moving pictures helped Jeanette escape her circumstances.

One December afternoon right before her twelfth birthday, Jeanette was listening to the large radio Arthur had bought that sat in their front room. Years later she wouldn't remember what she was listening to, only the serious news broadcaster who broke in telling them the Japanese had bombed Pearl Harbor. Jeanette was sure the world was coming to an end. The thought that Japan could invade the United States was bone-chilling. No matter how Inas attempted to reassure her daughter, it didn't work. She still used her rubber pacifier in secret, never outside the house. The kids poked too much fun at her, and being seen with a pacifier would seal her fate. But in that chaotic moment when her strong mother showed a crack in her reserve, with tears in her eyes, Jeanette was sure bombers were hovering over their house, and the pacifier was her only comfort.

Jeanette was right about the ending of her secure world. Not long after the news of the attack, Arthur had to go back to Powder Springs, Georgia. He made arrangements for Inas to stay with his friends not too far from the home where he lived with his wife and kids. As hard as Inas had tried to cover up her affair with a married man, Jeanette knew. She was too young to understand first cousins were not supposed to love each other in that way. But as it is in many cases, Jeanette understood much more than Inas realized. She knew Inas was in love with Arthur. Her mother actually smiled sometimes when Arthur was around. She remembered theses smiles from the time Estell and JD were alive. Inas's smiles soothed Jeanette, and for this reason she tried to like Arthur. What alternative did she have? The victims of these type of relationships are the children. Surely Arthur's two sons knew what his father was doing as well. Arthur Jr was old enough to go to war. Could his absence be the reason Arthur brought Inas back to Georgia? Was he needed at home because his firstborn would soon leave his mother and brother for combat?

While staying with friends, Inas wore her fake smile and Jeanette began school at R. L. Osborne on Joyner Avenue. Jeanette, now thirteen, dropped her pacifier through a hole in the interior wall of her new home. The treasured calming and sleep aid fell out of reach. The year was 1942, and rationing had begun. When Inas attempted to replace the rubber pacifier, there were only wooden ones on the store shelves. Rubber, too, was being rationed. When she handed the new pacifier to Jeanette, she popped it in her mouth, sucked on it once, and spit it across the room. Finally she weaned herself from the pacifier.

During this time, Inas managed to get a job with Bell Bomber—as a Rosie the Riveter—working on fighter planes. The plant would become Lockheed Martin after the war was over. Arthur probably had some influence on Inas getting the job, and she made more money than she could have imagined. Soon, the two of them went looking for a house. The normal place to begin this search was close to Jeanette's school. Inas's hours were long and Jeanette was spending a lot of time at home alone. If the school was close by, this would make her walk easier.

The house that caught Inas's eye was straight across from the school and the only one on Joyner Avenue for as far as she could see. The streetcar was less than a mile away, making the commute to work convenient. A couple owned the white, wood-sided house. The husband had been shipped to war. The wife planned to go stay with her parents and sold the house to Inas completely furnished. The thrilling prospect of having her own home was dashed when all the banks rejected her application for a loan. She made good money, but this didn't matter. The bank manager explained that even if she had cash, he would refuse her. Like many men, he believed women couldn't buy houses on their own. Arthur got the mortgage in his name, and Inas decided right then and there to pay a house payment each week from her paycheck until she paid it off. Only then could she get the deed in her name. She must have wondered what would happen if Arthur decided to stay with Mattie and not see Inas any longer. He had come home from South Carolina. What if Mattie found out about the house and insisted Inas and Jeanette move away? Inas had to pay off the house and make it hers. The cost was $2,500.00. Each week Inas took twenty-four dollars from her pay. She was paid sixty cents an hour and worked around forty-nine hours a week. Her weekly check was around twenty-nine dollars. This left her five dollars a week to buy food and pay for coal and electricity. Many nights Inas and Jeanette had cornbread and milk for dinner. On more than one occasion, there was only enough food for Jeanette. But in April 1943, Inas paid off the house. Inas pressured Arthur to have the deed changed into her name. To do this, she had to prove who she was. The bank wanted her marriage certificate to JD. Inas had anticipated this, and in March before she paid off the house, she obtained a photo of her birth record and went to the courthouse in Cobb County. She remembered clearly that when she and JD got their marriage certificate, the clerk had written her name as Susie and their last name as Loyd. Because JD could not read, he didn't see the mistakes. The produced birth record was used to correct Inas's first name, but the last name remained Loyd. Inas legally had a new last name and became a Loyd instead of a Lord. She went so far as to put "JD Loyd" on JD's headstone when she purchased one for his grave in the late forties. Her late baby daughter, Jeneva Estell, became a Loyd too.

Arthur remained a large presence in Jeanette's life. Many nights Inas would leave with him and come back near morning. By this point, Jeanette knew what her mother was doing. Many times she had been awakened by the two having sex in the front seat of Arthur's large Buick while she was supposed to be sleeping on the back seat.

Often I wonder when Jeanette's mental illness began to reveal itself. Surely signs were creeping into her everyday life as she battled her reality in contrast to the normalcy experienced by her schoolmates.

Stone 20

Walk

When the war ended in 1945, the country's cheers could be heard around the world. Jeanette was sixteen years old and living what would be the happiest part of her childhood. Inas had reconciled with her sister-in-law Corine and visited on a regular basis. Her younger sister, Stella Mae, had married a Fouts and lived just down the road from Ernest and Corine. Jeanette was reunited with her cousins Audrey and Doris once again. They also spent time with Grace, Clyde's daughter. Teenagers are teenagers no matter the time period. The Hawkins family had produced a clan of cousins around the same age. Jeanette suddenly had many friends, both female and male. She lived for the weekends when she visited Audrey. Her life on Joyner Avenue with a few friends—Nell, Martha, and Polly—was overshadowed by the exciting fun taking place in Newtown. Jeanette wanted to live there again. She longed for the family that disappeared when she was young. There with her extended family, she felt normal. Even though Uncle Ernest always made himself scarce when Inas came around, even though Jeanette knew Inas wouldn't approve of her feelings, even though Inas gave up everything to get her only daughter away from Newtown, Jeanette fell for the place where she had a real family. Her relationship with Ernest was a good one. Surely Jeannette knew the real reason her uncle handed Inas an ultimatum: not a possible tonsillectomy but a scandalous affair.

Ernest disapproved of Inas's choices and wanted nothing to do with them, but he respected his wife's love of his sister and allowed Inas to visit. And I have to believe a part of him loved his younger sister very much. He also wanted to influence Jeanette as much as he could.

By the time Inas came back to Newtown for visits, tragedy had hit Ernest and Corine. On June 12, 1943, the couple's daughter, Pamela Ann, was born. She lived twelve days. Corine had Rh negative blood. Pamela was born with Rh positive blood.* In 1943 doctors didn't know enough about the condition, and many babies died or the mothers had miscarriages.† The death of Pamela was tragic for the whole family but especially for big sister Audrey, who held the baby in her lap as Ernest rushed to the hospital in Atlanta.‡ The baby died shortly after they arrived at the emergency room. When Ernest and Corine's last daughter, Vickie Sue, was born in 1949, doctors knew to give her a blood transfusion and saved her life.

Jeanette not only spent many weekends with Audrey in Newtown but also brought Audrey to her house in Marietta, Georgia, for long stretches in the summer. Arthur allowed the girls to drive his Buick. This is how Jeanette learned to drive. They spent days in the backyard sunbathing in their new swimsuits, planning what they would do when they finished high

---

* The absence or presence of the blood protein Rh can lead to runaway immune reactions in Rh-positive babies born to mothers with Rh-negative blood.

† It wasn't until 1947 that doctors began to speak of preventive treatments for newborns with Rh disease. Newborns had transfusions of Rh-negative blood like their mothers. At the time, this procedure was not widely available.

‡ This event is recorded in the family archive.

school. Who would they marry? Neither spoke of college. Doris had graduated and was working at Southern Railway. She drove Ernest's car to the trolley stop in Brookhaven. Jeanette and Audrey often rode with Doris and spent the day walking the sidewalks and shopping the stores in downtown Atlanta. Sometimes they caught a movie before heading home. This is where Jeanette's passion grew for all kinds of movies. Many weekends found Jeanette and Audrey catching the trolley near Inas's house to Marietta Square to see the latest scary movie at the Strand Theater. When the movie was over, the girls caught the trolley back home. The stop was a mile from Inas's house. When the girls got off the trolley, they ran as fast as they could for home, fearing that the one of the movie monsters might be hiding in the shadows, waiting to catch them.

Inas lost her job at Bell Bomber like the majority of women hired during the war. The soldiers were coming home, and jobs had to be created for them. Inas's stomach knotted at the thought of losing her income. For the first time in her life, she made enough money to support herself and felt free to do what she wanted. This time she decided to find her own job instead of letting Arthur get one for her. A friend at Bell Bomber, also losing her job, told Inas that Rich's Department Store in downtown Atlanta was hiring. Inas asked Jeanette, who outshined her at the sewing machine many times over, to make her a black dress suit. When Jeanette finished, the pieces looked store bought.

"You should become a seamstress." Inas smiled at her.

Jeanette couldn't believe her ears. Inas never praised her. There had to be a catch. Usually, Inas only offered ways for her to improve. Now she had encouraged her daughter to pursue a job. Jeanette smiled back at Inas, but deep down she knew Inas only gave this suggestion because she didn't believe Jeanette could get a husband.

Jeanette urged her mother to splurge on a new pair of black heels, bought in the very store where she would go for the job interview. Whether it was the suit, the new shoes, or Inas's elegant reserve, the job was hers. But with this success came attachments. Rich's held their "girls" to high standards in dress, performance, and morals. Inas would have to keep Arthur a secret from her workplace supervisors and colleagues. Part of Inas loved the thought of hiding him instead of the other way around. Her work uniform was black skirts and white blouses. Not long after she began work, she received a promotion to assistant department manager. The pay was much lower than at Bell Bomber, but her house was hers and life required a little less money without a mortgage payment. In the beginning, Inas rode the street car to Atlanta each morning. She was the employee always ready to fill in for anyone who couldn't be there and was often paid for extra hours. Her upstanding attitude and work ethic in the large store became widely known. Her store discount allowed her to buy clothes for Jeanette and herself, but Inas was by no means a frivolous person. She opened a savings account, and each week she placed as much of her money there as she could manage.

Jeanette, now in her last year of high school, still struggled with acceptance, but the jeers and eye-rolling of her earlier years when she walked down the halls had become rare. Polly, her bravest, closest friend from school, insisted that she and Jeanette go to the sock hops alone. Jeanette's hobble disappeared when she danced, so it didn't take long for her to be the first to kick off her shoes, grab a friend, and dance until the band stopped playing. One of her favorite songs was "Chattanooga Choo Choo" by the Andrews Sisters. When Jeanette danced her heart out, she felt normal like all the other girls. She finally fit with in the crowd. She dropped her guard and enjoyed her newfound acceptance.

One afternoon the senior class practiced their graduation walk on the large front lawn of the school. The principal stood by observing. When Jeanette made her walk, she only wobbled slightly. She was more confident and less worried about her handicap. But then the principal dropped the papers he held and marched across the lawn to Jeanette.

"You, you." He pointed a finger at her.

Jeanette stood still. What had she done?

"Walk straight. This will be your graduation ceremony. You must be proud and give your best for the school."

Jeanette's fair skin turned red with embarrassment.

"Now try it again."

Part of hiding her hobble involved carefully placing her weight on the "good" leg, but the ground was soft from a previous night rain. As she walked toward her place in line, her limp was worse than ever.

"What is wrong with you?" the principal yelled. "Are you mocking me? Walk straight and stop that infernal limping, or come to my office where we will make a phone call to your parents."

Jeanette took two more steps.

"This is how you walk," he screamed at Jeanette, and he began to imitate her limp as he made a tight circle. "Young lady, what is your name?"

"Her name is Jeanette Loyd, and she can't help she walks like that. She was born that way." This was Polly, her protector, standing up to the principal.

Jeanette didn't dare look at her tormentor, but she heard him draw in a deep breath. "Does she have to walk? What a shame this would be for the class." He must have been speaking to his secretary.

"She has every right to walk," Polly insisted. "She's as good or better than the rest of us."

Jeanette finally looked at her friend. For the rest of her life, she would be indebted to her and trust her completely.

"You, young lady, may not walk." The principal came to stand in front of Jeanette. "Do you really want to ruin everyone's graduation with your hobble?"

When Jeanette looked into this man's eyes, she saw all the shame she had felt her whole life. She opened her mouth to agree with him, but Polly beat her to the answer.

"She will walk, or no girl in this class will walk." Polly wore her determined expression. Jeanette knew all the girls would do what she said out of pure fear.

"There will be no rebel-rousing in this school." But the principal walked back inside, followed by his secretary.

Polly looked at the group of seniors. "Anyone that has a problem with Jeanette walking in graduation, see me."

Even the boys turned and left.

"We're telling your mom." Polly took Jeanette by the arm.

"It would be easier to just not be part of the graduation." Jeanette said this with conviction. She wanted to walk away from school, quit right then, be through with the whole business.

When Polly told Inas later that evening about the incident, Inas's anger—most of the time tamed and hidden—flared. "No one will keep you from your graduation. No one."

She stared at her daughter. "You're a grown woman. You can't let men push you around like that. You have to stand up to them."

"I don't want to do it. I never did. Everyone will look at me." Jeanette knew she sounded childish, but her raw feelings surged out of her. "I've been made fun of my whole life. Haven't you noticed? Sometimes I wish had died instead of my sister. She had nothing wrong with her."

"Shut up," Inas screamed. "You will walk. You will be proud of who you are. I will see this man in the morning." Inas looked at Polly. "Thank you, young lady."

Later that night, Jeanette heard Inas talking to Arthur in the living room. "We are as good as any family at that school. I am going to see him."

Arthur spoke in his quiet way. "I will go with you."

"Is that a good idea?"

"Yes. His son works for me. I am your first cousin. I handle your affairs since you are widowed. I have an interest in my second cousin's welfare."

And Jeanette fell asleep not sure if having Arthur's support was a good thing or a bad thing. She had seen how he looked at Audrey and her when they wore bathing suits outside in the backyard. Of course Inas never noticed anything. In so many ways, Jeanette thought, Inas wasn't smart at all.

No matter how it actually came to pass, Jeanette did walk in her graduation and received her diploma.

Stone 21
Finally Love

The sepia photos of Jeanette as a teenager reveal a beautiful young woman. When placed side by side in chronological order, these images allow me to follow her growth and see her carefree relationship with her cousins in Newtown. She was having real fun. Audrey and Jeanette had always been best friends, and when they reunited, the two picked up where they left off. Many of the photos show them modeling matching clothes that Jeanette had made. A few are Hollywood-like shots of the girls lounging in front of Inas's house, bursting at the seams to be grown and on their own.

Then Audrey met a handsome boy named Ralph. The two fell in love. How they met is not clear since Ralph didn't go to school with Audrey and lived in Douglasville some forty miles west of Newtown. Maybe he shopped in the family store while working. Ernest had broken his back and moved from his large farm and house, renting it to his younger brother Clyde and his family. Moonshine, while still popular, wasn't the money-maker it had been a few years before. So Ernest bought a home with some land and a second house that he turned into a store. This was not far from Mt. Pisgah, the church the family had attended when Ernest was still at home and not yet married. Ernest and Corine had six children, five girls and one son, Lawrence, the next to youngest. The older kids, like Audrey, helped with the store. When Audrey began dating Ralph, she found Jeanette a date—a good girl always had another couple along. The photos show daytime outings with two different boys.

One, Earl Fouts, is snuggled up against Jeanette while the two stand on an old suspension bridge with the Chattahoochee River rushing underneath. In these photos, Jeanette's handicap is invisible. There is no uneven stance because of her leg. She is beautiful in her stylish print skirt wrapped around a small waist.

Audrey loved visiting her Aunt Inas, who had the latest clothes and makeup, not to mention a radio that the girls were allowed to listen to anytime they wanted. Back in Newtown, the girls had to fight for a chance to listen to Ernest's radio. Inas was forward thinking and beautiful. She allowed Ralph to visit as long as he did so when Inas was at home. So the girls switched houses each weekend.

Another group of photos shows Jeanette with a man named Paul Watkins. In each picture, the couple is dressed as if they have been to church. Paul wears a white dress shirt, creased dress pants, and a dark tie. His haircut is spot on and professional. In all these photos, Jeanette is wearing store-bought dresses, probably purchased by Inas at Rich's with her employee discount. Her two-tone heels flatter her shapely legs. The possessive hand at her waist shows that Paul cares for Jeanette, and her confidence shows in her genuine smile.

Jeanette graduated from R. L. Osborne, walking down the aisle to receive her diploma from the very man who had questioned her right to do so. It was done. She was grown up. Audrey graduated too and married Ralph shortly after graduation. Jeanette did not attend her best friend/cousin's graduation or wedding. Instead, she went on a trip with her girlfriends from high school, Polly, Martha, and Nell. Inas was infuriated with this plan, but for the first time in her life Jeanette stood up against her mother. There is a grainy sepia 8-millimeter home movie showing the girls on a dock in Daytona Beach, Florida. Polly is holding a claw of a crab, swinging the poor creature toward her friends, who squeal. From that trip forward, Inas would not like Polly. That movie captures the youth of these women at a time in their lives when the world was theirs. They didn't know the future, just the happy trip and being with the closest of friends.

Polly married a local bad boy who later crashed his car at 120 mph into a bridge abutment and died, leaving her with a baby son that she had named after him. Shortly after, Polly married a man who became the fire chief at Lockheed Martin. They built a beautiful house on two acres of land at the end of Joyner Avenue. The property boasted a three-bedroom, two-bath house, a house-sized screened-in building with two large brick barbecue pits, and several picnic tables. The screen house was wired for lights, and many parties were thrown.* A large glass greenhouse stood on the back portion of the property, where Polly's husband grew all kinds of plants and vegetables.†

Jenelle and Martha were sisters living with an abusive father who beat them. Both married as soon as possible. Martha remained married and had two boys and a girl. Jenelle married and divorced several times, even landing on Inas's sofa more than once.

Instead of following in the path of friends and marrying Paul Watkins, Jeanette went to work at the Atlanta Gas Company. Along the way she met a flashy solider in the Air Force who was twenty-nine, Glover Allen Swafford. She was almost twenty, and finally she found true love, but at what price?

---

* After coming home from Germany, I would have sleepovers with Polly's youngest daughter in this building.

† As children, we would find his hiding place for beer tucked into a cooler under the planting tables.

Stone 22
They Live Happily Ever After

The Swafford family can be traced back to England in 1662 when two Quaker brothers immigrated to what would become Pennsylvania. Glover Swafford's family thread began in North Georgia with his great-grandfather Isaac Newtown Swafford—who originally lived on Hog Mountain in Gwinnett County, Georgia, with his wife Ailey Ann Bailey—moved to Ellijay, Georgia, after he came home from the Civil War.* Glover Allen was born in Altoona, Bartow County, Georgia, on March 8, 1920. He was one of eight children, six girls and two boys, himself and Tallmage, his younger brother by three years. In 1937—the middle of the Depression—Glover joined the CCC at seventeen years old. Part of FDR's administration, this agency was a godsend for many young men all over the country. Glover worked outside, building parks and roads in Georgia and Alabama. He received three meals a day with much larger portions that he was accustomed to eating in his struggling family. He actually gained weight in the years he was in the CCC. He received a dollar a day, and this was sent home to his family to help them put food on the table.

When World War II began after the bombing of Pearl Harbor, most of the young men in the CCC went directly into

---

* Isaac Newtown Swafford enlisted in the Civil War in September 1861. On October 13, 1861, while in Virginia he deserted and swore allegiance to the Union Army and fought for them. This is why he never returned to Hog Mountain.

the military. Glover had enlisted at Gunter Field in Montgomery, Alabama, on November 25, 1941, in the Army Air Corps,† two weeks before Pearl Harbor. He was twenty-one. His career began that day. He served in World War II, Korea, and Vietnam, not to mention many classified Cold War projects. This man, my father, instilled in me a love of country and honor, and a passion for history. Not once did he tell a gruesome experience to get his point across. Instead, he used a subtleness I would understand only as an adult.‡

How does a daughter go through most of her life without knowing how her parents met? Mother was forthcoming with information on where they married and what they wore, but she never told me how she met Dad. In March 2019, I found my half-sister, who is seventy-three to my sixty-one. I always knew Dad was married before Mother, and he had another daughter and son. I never met them, or so I was led to believe.

---

† The Air Force wasn't founded as an independent branch of the military until 1947 when President Truman signed the National Security Act.

‡ While we were living in Germany, our family went on a trip to Austria. While my mother and little brother remained at the hotel, Dad took me with him on a sightseeing visit. The year was 1966, only twenty-one years after World War II ended. Many of the memorials had not been established yet. We entered a deserted area with a large brick arch and a heavy chain across the opening. The grass was tall, but we made our way to a grass-covered bunker. Dad looked down the steps into the room under the ground. The door was open, and natural light spilled in enough to show me block walls. The very air was thick, desolate, sad. I asked my dad what this place was. He told me it was a place where German soldiers did bad things to people who didn't deserve to be punished. When I was an adult, I saw a room just like this on a documentary: a gas chamber in a concentration camp. When I called Mother, she explained it was Mauthausen in Austria, and Dad had been part of the liberation. He wanted me to see this place, knowing one day I would get the meaning.

In my first conversation with my sister, she told me there was a photo of her holding me when I was a baby. A few conversations later, she told me that Mother had met our dad while he was married to her mother. The family was living in Georgia not far from Mother. I will never know where Mother actually met Dad, but he was married, and they dated for a while before he left his first wife and shipped out to serve in the Korean War sometime around 1951 and returned in 1953. Inas saw his infidelity as a strike against Glover from the moment Jeanette brought him home—in Jeanette's favor, Inas didn't like anyone who took her daughter away from her own influence. Could Jeanette's mental illness have begun to show up at that time? She was twenty-four.

Jeanette and Glover exchanged letters throughout the Korean War.[§] The two were married at City Hall on the square in Marietta, Georgia, on May 22, 1954. Jeanette wore a cream-colored suit she made. Glover bought her a string of pearls and these hung around her neck. Glover wore his dress uniform. Jeanette used her paycheck to buy him a yellow-gold wedding band. Jeanette was given Inas's wedding band from her marriage to JD. The newlyweds spent their honeymoon at the Historic Kennesaw House, also on the Marietta Square. Glover left three days later for Warner Robins Air Force Base near Macon, Georgia. Jeanette followed as soon as Glover found a house to rent.

The photos of Jeanette around the time she began seeing Glover reflect a sober young woman, not a carefree youth. In

---

[§] When I was eighteen, the man who handled my car insurance recognized my father's name as the buddy he had served with in Korea. He told me a story of a Korean woman Dad fell in love with while there. He was very surprised that they did not marry.

all the photos, even ones with Glover, she wears a troubled expression, as if she isn't completely present or doing her best to sort out some problems. Lost in a dark depth is a good description of her in these photos. Maybe she shouldered the guilt of being like Inas. In all likelihood, Glover married a young woman fighting mental illness or at the very least depression. Inas had lost control of her daughter, and this was distressing to her. She did not approve of the marriage.**

Jeanette and Glover had a girl on December 9, 1957, at the base in Warner Robins. Glover signed his daughter's birth certificate. That baby girl was me. Within nine months, Glover received new orders and his small family moved to Newport News, Virginia, leaving behind his two children from his first marriage.

** After Granny died, Mother told me she believed Granny and my father, Glover, had an affair. At the time, I considered this another one of her paranoid stories. But I was always bothered by her passion and hate-filled tone when she told this story to me.

Part Seven

Ann, 1959–1965

Stone 23
My Little Doll

I loved my daddy best, hands down. We lived in Virginia. Mama was a wild card—that's what Daddy said in a joking way, but I knew he was not joking, not really. He had seen her get mad and throw a fit, but he didn't know how she acted while he was away at work. I never knew when I would get a spanking for something. The rules changed from day to day. We lived on a street close to the Southwest Branch Back River that separated us from Langley Air Force Base, where Daddy worked. This is the first home I can remember. Mama said we lived in Georgia before that, but I can't recall the house there. Mama decorated my room as a nursery when we first moved to Virginia, and all I remember is looking into floating birds of all colors above me. My favorite was the cardinal. I kept that bird on my bookshelf long after the crib mobile was taken down. I loved cardinals because Mama was partial to what she called red birds.

"When you see a red bird, Ann, it means someone is visiting you from Heaven."

I wondered who she hoped was visiting. Maybe her daddy because he died when she was young. She told me about him dying one day like it was a secret that we shouldn't share. I remember sleeping in my baby bed in the nursery, and I remember the day Mama replaced it with a single bed in the middle of the floor like an island in the ocean. Beautiful curtains and a bedspread covered in roses were the prettiest things in my room. I wasn't sure why I had a fancy room. Mama wouldn't let me play with my toys because playing messed up the neat floors and shelves. She liked perfect. At night I slept with her while Daddy slept in my bed. He didn't like my room one bit and fussed on some mornings, telling me I was too big of a girl to sleep with Mama. He was right, but I was scared in the dark. Daddy gave Mama the most beautiful things for the kitchen. We had some plates and cups just like the ones on one of my favorite TV shows, *I Love Lucy*. The pattern was green ivy vines running all over a cream-colored background. Daddy also gave Mama fancy dinner glasses that made me think of diamonds. I loved diamonds, shiny and sparkly. Mama didn't have any real diamonds, just a gold band. I decided that when I grew up, I would marry a man who bought me a big diamond that sparkled in the light.

Mama saved green stamps from our grocery trips. When she filled a lot of books with these stamps, we went to the green stamp store and traded them in for a mixer with shiny metal bowls, lamps for the living room, and, for me, a beautiful bride doll and a Shirley Temple doll dressed in a red polka dot dress with black dress shoes. I was allowed to hold the Shirley Temple doll only sometimes. I couldn't hug her or play with her. The bride doll was only for looks and sat on my bed. No touching. But sometimes when Mama wasn't around, I touched the veil covering the doll's face. One day I wanted to wear one of those in my own wedding.

Mother had a yellow 1957 Chevy, and Daddy used a scooter to go back and forth to work each day, crossing the long bridge over the river. Of course, if it was raining he took our car. Each afternoon as the time got close for him to come home, I stood at the screen door to watch. When he arrived, I ran to stand on the running board of the scooter while Daddy gave me a ride around the neighborhood. Home was always a good place when he was there.

Pretending was my favorite game. I pretended a lot of things. I invented friends to play with because Mama didn't let me play with the kids next door. Daddy said I was an observer, a gatherer of feelings and a studier of body language. I didn't know what that meant, but when he said it, I felt important, not just the bad child who got in trouble with Mama all the time. I was smarter than most kids my age, and I talked like an adult. Daddy said I was around grownups too much. But I liked them the best. I watched Daddy when Mama talked about cooking a new recipe, how he snuck in an eye-roll when she wasn't looking at him. Eye-rolling showed contempt—that's what Mama told me when she caught me doing the same thing. Mama stiffened straight like a tall pine tree when Daddy gave her excuses of why he had to be late, once again, for supper.

I told myself stories that wove around, springing alive, keeping me company during the long naps Mama forced me to take each day. She slept beside me, her breath heavy but fluid, a soft-moving creek. The lines across her forehead smoothed. During those naps, I saw her real face, the one she hid from Daddy and the whole world. She looked young when she slept, like a little girl.

If the truth was told, I loved being alone. It wasn't so bad, though I was afraid of just about anything. Simple things other kids didn't worry over. If the wind blew too hard, I thought the roof would blow away and then the house might crumble to the ground. The dark hall at night that led to my room was a terrifying place. If monsters lived in our house, the hall was their home. Mama laughed at me sometimes, saying I was a fraidy-cat. Daddy never laughed. He thought I was silly and weak, and he didn't like weak. Thunder and lightning scared me a lot, but at least Mama was scared too. My hair being rinsed in the tub with large cups of water poured over my face made me scream. My empty bedroom when it was time to go to bed made me cry. The shadows in the corners.

Daddy thought I was smart to memorize his hand of cards when he taught me to play gin rummy. He called me a genius. Daddy often gave me praise because I read my favorite books without missing one word. Mama said I memorized them like I did his cards, that I wasn't reading, but she was wrong. I knew the words. I liked words even back then.

Mama and Daddy didn't yell and scream, not much, not at each other. I think things would have been less confusing had they done this. But no, the bad things that happened in the house always took place when I slept. That's when Mama cried. I would squeeze my eyes closed in her big bed and think about being a princess in a castle. I believed in magic, good and bad. All kids do. I was sure something bad—like a ghost or witch—lived in the shadows, waiting to trip up Daddy and especially Mama. I believed a world took place right alongside my life, day in and day out. And on the bad, scary days, I prayed hard that my world would explode and blow all the bad to bits. I believed in Heaven—still do—and Hell because the preacher at our church said these places existed.

When I was an adult, Mother gave me an old black-and-white photo taken at that house in Virginia. In the photo, my parents are sitting on a sofa half smiling. I sit between them, holding the straps of my purse—I so wanted to be a grown woman. My smile is large because Daddy's old war buddy is taking the photo. I was quite taken with him because he laughed and talked to me. The cracked and creased photo doesn't reflect what was really taking place in that house. The image is, in many ways, a lie. The energy, the undercurrent, the flow between my parents was an electrical charge sure to catch fire at some point.

My first memory of Mama is her scent. White Shoulders, the perfume, lingered on and soaked into all the surfaces in our house, bleeding through our clothes, furniture, carpets, and my toys, bedsheets, drapes. Mama's essence—the mixture of her genes with mine—was soft movements, an unheard music that completed me. On some days, Mama and I were one person moving to the same tune.

I remember sitting in my baby bed—looking through the wooden bars—and seeing a large brown dog with fluffy hair and a sharp nose barking and growling at me. No one else was in the room. I cried. The dog kept growling and barking. Mama always said there was no way I should be able to recall this because it happened in Georgia, and she gave the dog away when I was nine months old. She said I must have heard her talking about the day this dog jumped at my bed, intent on biting me. But I still remember the scene my way, vivid in intricate details.

Some of my happiest and saddest memories were made in the Virginia house. The days were lazy and long with Mama and me together around the clock. Around the clock. Mama said this like it drove her crazy. Around the clock. She never left me with a sitter so she could go out with friends. Women didn't come for coffee or tea. Mama hated drinking hot beverages. Mama was different, really different—not like Daddy, who spoke in a quiet, solid voice, a man a little girl could believe. Trust.

Mama made me dolls and doll clothes. She loved sewing the best, better than she loved me and Daddy, and she sat at her sewing machine all day. The very act made her the happiest. Thinking back, I recognize my obsessive passion for writing in the way she worked on her sewing projects, as if this act defined her, completed her as a person. The Kenmore sewing machine Daddy bought her sat on a card table in their bedroom. Some days I made my way under the table to play with the homemade dolls and be close to her. When Mama pressed what looks like a gas pedal in a car, the sewing machine engine vibrated through the metal legs into the wooden floor. Many times I fell into a deep sleep, like Snow White after she bites the poison apple, while waiting for Mama to finish working and get us lunch. On sunny warm days, she put me in the fenced backyard and locked the screen door so I couldn't bother her while she worked. The yard was huge, with flowering bushes sitting under the windows of the house. I pretended to be a queen, and the swing set became a castle on one day and an airplane on another. Oh, the stories I acted out. But finally my mouth turned dry and my stomach rumbled. I yelled through the screen for Mama to let me in, but the only answer that came back was the sound of the sewing machine humming away at full speed. Often times I peed my panties because I couldn't get to the bathroom. The first time it happened, I hung the wet underwear on a large azalea bush to dry in the sun. Mama happened to unhook the door and call me inside before I put them back on.

"Ann, where are your panties?" Her tone turned cold and angry. "Why are you out here in the backyard dancing around with no clothes?"

"I'm wearing my clothes," I said.

Her face turned into a black thunderstorm cloud. "Don't talk back. Only nasty girls go without their panties for all to see." She yanked my arm. "Is that what you want to be, a nasty girl?"

"No." The grip stung my arm.

"When are you going to be a big girl? Always wetting your pants." She held the damp underwear between two fingers away from her. "Get to the bathroom and sit on the potty until you're told to get up. If you are going to wet your clothes, maybe you don't need the new dress I'm making. I should just spank you."

I hurried to the dark bathroom, tiled in blue. It was the darkest room in the house besides the hall. I sat on the wooden potty chair with the lamb appliqué on the back.

"Now you sit there until you pee and decide not to wet your pants again." The window in the bathroom was open, and the kids in the house behind us—where a large, very overweight woman watched children to make extra money—ran out of the screen door, slamming it a bunch of times, yelling and laughing. I wanted to be in the yard with them. Happy. Mama refused to allow me out of the backyard. I wasn't allowed to play with children I didn't know. I wondered if those kids were ever locked out of the house like me. How did they hold their pee for so long?

Sitting on the potty seemed to stretch into hours. Mama stuck her head in the door. "Have you used the bathroom?"

"No." I needed a drink.

"You can't get up until you do." She shut the door again.

That's when I got the best idea. I stood on my tiptoes and turned on a trickle of water, letting it fall into the bathroom cup. I poured it in the potty, put the cup back, and sat down.

"I'm finished," I yelled.

Her footsteps came down the hall and she opened the door. "Stand up."

I did.

"Now, look what a big girl you can be when you want." Her smile was warm, forgiving. She always bragged to everyone, even when I was an adult, that she had me potty trained by the time I was six months old. She took great pride in my bathroom habits. "Wipe yourself and go watch TV. *Bandstand* is on. We will eat lunch in a minute."

Mama and I watched this show every afternoon, and if she was in a good mood, we danced along with the teenagers on the screen. "Before I married your dad, I was a good dancer," she said. In that moment I would have believed anything. She taught me to twirl to the song "Venus" as we moved around the living room. When she danced, her limp was gone. She was happy.

I loved music because of Mama. She bought me a portable record player with a bunch of 45 rpm records that I listened to in my room. Sometimes she yelled, "I can't hear that song again, Ann."

So I changed the record. My prized possession was an album by Bobby Vinton, *Roses Are Red*. I loved every song and listened to them over and over. Sometimes Mama came into my room and stretched out on the bed. She hummed with her eyes closed, smiling like she was somewhere else rather than listening to the music with me.

September 1960

One afternoon Daddy called from work to say he had to stay on base. A hurricane was supposed to hit, Hurricane Donna. Mama was terrified. "Please, Glover, what are we supposed to do? Should I drive inland?" Daddy must have said no because we never left the house.

For supper Mama heated TV dinners in shiny foil trays, and we ate them in front of the television. This seemed like the perfect evening, but Mama only watched the news. Over and over the man told what could happen to all of us in the path of the hurricane. When the weather turned windy, we crawled into Mama's bed, where she read *Little Women* out loud. Mama didn't like to read, but she saw on TV that if she read the classic books to me, I would be intelligent. We fell asleep to the wind howling. I was safe with Mama.

We woke up the next morning to the storm still raging outside. Mama was scared. "Where is your father?" She tried to use her aggravated voice, but I could see straight through her act. Our phone rang, and Mama grabbed the receiver.

"Hello." She listened and looked out the large picture window. "Our street is dry but there are trees down and the house down the road is missing part of the roof." She listened again. "That is horrible. We will hear from them soon. I know we will. Be careful and don't go out yet. The storm is still bad. Okay. Bye."

"Who was that?" I stood at her elbow.

She looked down at me. "A woman whose husband works with your father. She wanted to know how bad the road is here. She hasn't heard from her husband, and she is worried." We stood beside each other, quiet. Mama gave a shudder. "That bridge is probably gone."

After the storm moved away, the man across the street came to tell us that two streets over, people had to get in rowboats and canoes to leave their homes. Power had gone out for mostly everyone, but we still had lights. Windows and signs were broken and flattened. Not far from us at Huntington Park, Red's Pier—one of Daddy's favorite places—was nearly destroyed. The neighbor's news just frightened Mama more.

She picked up the phone to try Daddy again. The line was dead, but she tried to make it work over and over.

At lunchtime, Mama got out cheese. "We're going to have grilled cheese sandwiches. Perfect for a rainy day."

I wasn't hungry, but I didn't say this. I got in my chair and waited.

Just as Mama opened a can of chicken noodle soup to go with our sandwiches, we heard a car. I ran to the window. "It's a truck." Then I saw my daddy get out. "It's Daddy!" But Mama was already out the door.

She cried big sobs for all the neighbors in their yards and windows to see, and I wrapped my arms around his neck as he picked me up.

In the kitchen I sat in his lap, and Mama pulled her chair close. Daddy told us that even though the storm hit at low tide, the fierce northwesterly waves and winds caused a lot of damage.

"No one on the other side of the bridge could make it across because of the flooding. I can't believe there is no flooding on this road." He looked out the window again.

I almost asked how he made it across the river without the bridge, but I decided the story would be too scary.

We had TV dinners in the living room again in honor of

Daddy being safe and sound. My parents laughed and talked. They even allowed me to fall asleep in the living room close to them. We were all ok. This wasn't true for everyone.*

Mother's reading to me made me want more. I loved any kind of stories. My favorite story was *Peter Pan*. Mother took me to see the Disney version in the theater and bought me the soundtrack album of the whole movie. I listened to it so much I knew all the character voices and lines. And of course, I wanted to be Peter instead of Wendy. After all, he could fly and fight off all the bad guys. He had a sword! Tiger Lily liked him. And best of all, he was the captain of his own destiny, with no parents to tell him how to act. I loved Peter Pan so much that Daddy refused to tell the story at bedtime anymore. "We need a new story," he said. But I was in love with the thought of being so strong.

Mama showed me two tickets to see the "real" Peter Pan performed on a live stage. "We're going to see the stage play. You know Peter is always played by a woman?"

"Peter Pan is not a woman."

Mama laughed.

When we saw the play, I fell even more in love with the story if that was possible. "I want to be Peter Pan," I whispered to Mama.

---

* Fifty-seven years later, someone wrote about this storm in an article for the *Daily Press*. See Mark St. John Erikson, "Hurricane Donna Left 3 Dead in Hampton Roads on this Day in 1960," September 12, 2017, *Daily Press*, http://www.dailypress.com/features/history/dp-nws-hurricane-donna-1960-20150913-story.html.

"Don't you want to be Wendy?" Mama asked after listening to me go on and on about Peter.

"No. She doesn't do anything but ask for help."

"Well, you're a little girl. You will understand better when you get older. Women don't save the day, Ann. They are moms and wives."

I decided I didn't want to be like Mama. I wanted to do things for myself.

"You'll never get a husband acting like that," Mama fussed.

Daddy overheard. "Good. She doesn't need to be married."

Mama didn't open her mouth, but somehow I was sure this comment made her upset with Daddy and me.

Dinnertime became a real problem as I began to decide to eat what I liked, not what was good for me. Mama believed I should eat whatever she placed in front of me. Her favorite dish to make for Daddy—I think he hated it as much as me—was chicken and dumplings. I hated that watery, slimy concoction covered in pepper. The battle began as soon as I caught the scent of the despised dinner and ended with me sitting at the table long after Mama and Daddy left. The battle of wills always made Mama the winner, so I ended up forcing several soggy, cold bites down my throat, gagging with each one. When I finished, Mama sent me from the kitchen, without dessert, to my room for the night.

Mama's strictest food moments were always about sugar. No sweet cereal crossed the threshold of our door. I so longed for Tony the Tiger's Frosted Flakes, but instead I got the box with a dumb rooster on the front, Corn Flakes. When I knew Mama or Daddy were not around, I would slip two spoonfuls of sugar from the bowl that sat on the table. Instead of sprinkling them on my cereal, I shoved them in my mouth.

One day while shopping at Sears—the 1960s-style store was very different from today's—Mama stopped at their bakery to gaze into the glass candy case. I pointed to the bin of multi-colored coconut bonbons. "Please can we have some?"

In a completely weak moment, Mama agreed to buy a pound and handed me the white paper bag. "Two a day. That is it."

I chose two chocolate ones and ate them so fast I nearly missed the blast of sweet coconut filling my mouth. By the time we pulled into our drive at home, I was craving more.

Mama took the bag from me. "You can have two more tomorrow. Now go play. I have to change clothes." She was wearing a dress, bracelet, dress shoes, and a necklace. This is how women dressed when they went shopping in the sixties.

As soon as the door to her room clicked shut, I scooted my stool to the counter, took the white bag, and hid behind the door in my bedroom. I popped a red bonbon into my mouth and sucked. My intention was to eat only one piece. Mother would never know. But like any addict, I lost track of the pieces I ate. One after another after another. What heaven this candy was! The white bag was empty. I crumpled it and pushed it under my pillow. I ran outside, happy, content, to play on my swing.

Thank goodness we had my favorite supper. I ate two hot dogs, smothered in ketchup and mustard, and three heaping spoons of baked beans. Not long after dinner, my stomach began to rumble and shooting pains doubled me over. I cried out.

Mama came to the door of my room and gave me her half-angry look. "You know why you're sick. Follow me to the bathroom. I have something that will help."

I followed, moaning the whole way.

She measured a spoonful of liquid from a small brown bottle. "You have to take this medicine."

I swallowed the nasty-tasting stuff and instantly vomited. Then I vomited again. This was worse than the stomachache.

Daddy came to the bathroom door. "What is wrong with her?"

Mama rubbed my head while I threw up again. "I had to give her syrup of ipecac. It makes her vomit up what is bothering her stomach."[†]

"Isn't that the same stuff they use when somebody swallows poison?" Daddy frowned.

"Yes, doctors use it for that too," Mama said in her testy voice. Daddy was crossing over into her territory—me. She never mentioned the candy, but we both knew I suffered a sufficient punishment for my lie.

Soon after this incident, Mama became obsessed over my bathroom habits. "You're not pooping every day. This isn't right. I think you are holding it just to spite me, Ann. These will keep you regular." She gave me two small brown pills at bedtime. I was forced to swallow them whole with some water. When I woke up the next morning, my stomach cramped, and I barely made it to the bathroom before I went.

Mama stuck her head in the door. "Good, the laxatives worked. I was worried the adult dose would be too much."

[†] Most households stocked this drug in the 1960s to induce vomiting after a child ingested poison. Later, doctors would reverse this advice and tell parents to remove it from their homes. See "Ipecac: Don't Use It!" Poison Control, https://www.poison.org/articles/ipecac-do-not-use-it.

My stomach cramped and hurt the rest of the day, sending me to the bathroom several times. The next day the pills didn't make me go as much. After a couple of months, the pills didn't bother me at all and I stopped going again. This made Mama add another pill, so I was taking four adult laxatives at a time.[‡] Mama must have worried about my intake because she began to give them to me three times a week instead of every night. Daddy never knew what Mama did to me on most days. It was easy for a young girl to think he didn't care and that he was too busy with work. As a little girl, I didn't see how Mama changed when he walked in the door, how she did a decent job at hiding her mental problems.

I loved to go into my room, shut the door, and turn on my music loud. Then I would get on my bed and jump. I jumped as high as I wanted and touched the ceiling. When I jumped, strength spread through me. This was almost as good as going outside to play with kids, but not quite.

One afternoon, I didn't hear the door open.

"What are you doing? You could break your neck. I've told you about jumping on the furniture." Mama crossed the room.

I jumped off the bed to get out of her range.

"Get over here. What have I told you?" She circled the bed.

I was trapped. The last thing I wanted was a spanking from her. She always used the nearest object. That day she held her hairbrush.

"You are a bad girl." She pointed the white brush at me.

[‡] This cycle continued throughout my childhood. My body became dependent on the laxatives. I was nineteen years old before I finally weaned myself off the use of this over-the-counter drug.

"This time your father is going to handle the spanking. Not me. I'm tired. You stay in your room and think about what you did. Leave this door open." She marched out.

I sat on the bed, happy that Daddy would handle my punishment. Daddy would be so disappointed with me for misbehaving.

Later that evening, Mama cooked Daddy's favorite: steak, baked potatoes, and green peas. I loved all this food except the peas, but I had learned to eat them anyway.

"Something smells good." Daddy entered my room and picked me up above his head.

"Mama cooked a good supper." I laughed.

"Glover." Mama stood in the doorway. "You have to give Ann a spanking. Use your belt. She was bad today."

Daddy put me down and gave me a sad look.

"Don't let her get away with disrespect." Mama left the door before he could argue with her.

"Wait here." Daddy shook his head and walked out of the room.

My heart banged around my chest. Was he really going to spank me?

"Glover, she is four years old. It's time for her to learn how to respect me," Mama called from the kitchen in a happy voice.

I stood by my bed, waiting. On the nightstand by the pink lamp was my favorite toy. Granny, whom I hadn't seen since I was a baby, had sent me a little girl witch candle for Halloween the previous year. Mama thought I was too young to have a candle, but she agreed to let me keep it as long as it was never lit. This was fine with me, since burning it would cause the witch hat to melt. I wanted to keep her perfect.

Daddy came into my room and shut the door. He wore

his green work uniform and big combat boots. He took off his belt.

Tears filled my eyes and blurred my vision.

"Turn around and bend over." Daddy folded the belt in half, holding the buckle parts in his hand. Mama always beat me with the buckle.

The belt hit my butt, and a sob escaped into the air, but not because it hurt that bad. Mama hit much harder. No, I was crying because I had spoiled things between Daddy and me. He hit me two more times, four total. "Look at me."

I turned and stared him in the face.

"Don't upset your mother again. You know how she is. Stay under the radar. Do you know what that means?"

I shook my head.

"Radar is a detection system that tracks planes and how close they are. In war, if a plane stays under the radar, the detection system, no one knows they are there. Stay under the radar with your mother. Don't give her a reason to look for a belt or get mad. Try to stay out of sight."

I wanted to say she always watched me, that staying under the radar with Mama was next to impossible.

He walked out of the room without ever knowing what I did to get a spanking. "Jeanette, don't ask me to do that again. I won't. Do you understand?"

"She is bad. I need your help. I don't know what to do to manage her."

Anger pushed through me, and before I stopped to think, I threw the pretty witch candle on the floor. It cracked in half, and I cried even harder.

Months Later

"Your granny is coming to visit," Mama said as she hung up the phone. "She is going to stay two weeks."

Daddy snuck in an eye-roll.

"And Glover, she is flying. Imagine flying to see us. Mother will do just about anything." Mama's tone of voice showed her pride in my grandmother. "You get to see your granny again," she said to me. "Aren't you happy?"

"She doesn't remember your mother, Jeanette," Daddy yelled from his chair in the living room. "She was a baby the last time your mother saw her."

"Well, I know that, but she sends Ann letters and gifts all the time. At least she thinks about her."

I knew Mama was hinting at how my other grandmother, Daddy's mama, didn't do that because I was the twenty-fifth grandchild. Granny, on the other hand, had only me. That made me pretty special.

"Mother will be here on Sunday. Can you help me pick her up?"

"Yes." Daddy's voice sounded tired.

We stood at the airport that Sunday, watching the plane my granny was on come to a stop. Two men rolled a tall set of stairs up to the door of the plane. I wished I could fly on a plane. That would have been better than jumping on my bed. The door swung open and a pretty lady with a dress and matching hat helped people onto the first step as I watched. Where was Granny? She probably had gray hair and looked old. Grannies were old. Lots of people began filing down the stairs, and family met them at the gate with hugs and kisses. Granny had probably missed the plane. Mother was watching the door like me. Daddy smoked and looked at everyone, especially the lady with blond hair standing down the line from us. He did this sometimes, watched pretty women. Mama never paid him any attention.

Mama squeezed my shoulder. "There she is, Ann. The woman with the blue coat."

This woman scanned the people standing behind the fence and stopped on us, throwing her hand up and moving as fast as she was allowed down the stairs. Mama took my hand and led me to the front of the gate. Daddy was left behind.

Granny's smile was shiny like the sun. She was the bravest woman in the world, flying in an airplane to Newport News. I waved as hard as I could. Granny laughed when she stood before us. She was young. Her hair was curly, brown, and cut close to her head. Her red lipstick made her beautiful and exotic.

She pulled me to her, smashing my face into her thigh. "Look at you. Pictures just don't do you justice. You look just like your mom when she was your age." She squatted. "I'm so happy to finally see you, Annie."

My cheeks heated. The name was perfect for me: Annie. "You are my doll," she added, then stood and gave Mama a look over.

This was my mama's mother. I couldn't imagine Mama as a kid.

Granny pulled Mama close in a hug. "It's been way too long, Jeanette."

No special name for Mama.

"I've missed you, Mother." Mama looked like she might cry.

Granny turned her attention on Daddy, who had caught

up to us. "Glover, you look good. Have you been taking care of my girls?"

"I always do," Daddy answered. He gave a half smile to Granny, then gathered her suitcase. We were off for home.

The first thing Granny did was take over the cooking. "Jeanette, can you drive me to the grocery store?"

Daddy rolled his eyes but nobody paid him any mind. "I'm going to watch golf." This was Daddy's favorite thing to watch on TV except for baseball. He loved baseball the best.

Mama drove, and Granny sat in the front beside her. I sat by the window in the back and listened to them talk about the people where Granny lived. When we parked in front of the store, Granny turned around to look at me. "I want you to pick out the fruit for our dessert. It will be a cobbler. Have you eaten this before?"

I shake my head.

"Don't you have a voice? Speak up, Annie, or no one will ever hear you."

"No."

"No ma'am." Mama said.

"No ma'am."

Granny nodded. "Then you are in for a treat. Now, what is your favorite supper?"

"Hot dogs or hamburgers," I yelled.

Granny frowned. "No, that won't do on Sunday. It has to be special."

I took a deep breath. "Fried chicken."

Granny smiled. "I love me some fried chicken. Do you like cornbread?"

"Yes ma'am. With lots of butter."

Granny opened the door for me. "Of course, it's not cornbread without butter."

Supper that night was the best I had ever eaten. The cobbler was peach with a scoop of vanilla ice cream that melted into a puddle right in the middle of the pie. I ate mine real slow to make it last a long time. Daddy had seconds of everything.

Granny put me to bed. "I'm going to sleep with you tonight. Will that bother you?"

"No ma'am."

Granny smiled. "Good. Let me do my girl stuff and I'll be right back to tell you a story. Be thinking of one."

"Ok." I snuggled into my pillow and left a lot of room for Granny. She didn't know I hated sleeping in my bed.

She appeared in the door a few minutes later, wearing a soft yellow robe and missing her glasses.

"Where's your glasses?" I asked.

She crawled in beside me. "I can't wear them to bed. I would break them rolling around."

I giggled.

"What story do you want?"

"I love *Peter Pan*."

She tucked her arm under my head, pulling me close. "Who wouldn't love *Peter Pan*? Who is your favorite character?"

"Peter and Tiger Lily."

"I'm partial to Captain Hook, myself."

I looked up at her. "You can't like him. He's the bad guy."

"Who says? What kind of story would it be without Captain Hook? He is by far the most interesting."

I thought about this for a minute. "I guess."

"I will tell the Captain Hook parts and you tell the Peter

Pan parts. It will be like doing a play."

"Yes. Yes."

Each morning Granny was out of bed first. She cooked breakfast. My favorite was pancakes and bacon. I used a lot of syrup, and Mama didn't say a word. She didn't fuss at me at all. She smiled a lot, and a few times Granny would shoo her away to go with Daddy to the officer's club while she and I stayed at home. It was like Granny had come to see just me, even though she did visit with Mama. They talked a lot. I pretended to nap beside Granny and listened to their talk.

"That's going to be a long way, Jeanette."

"I know, Mother, but we have no choice."

"I worry about you so far away from home."

"I will be fine."

Two weeks flew by, and it was time for Granny to leave.

"Get up, Annie. You have to take me to the airport. I'm going home."

The time with my granny had been better than Christmas. I didn't want her to leave. Mama had been nice to me the whole time and didn't give me one spanking. The food was so good that I looked forward to meals. No one had argued. And who was going to tell me stories like Granny?

I helped her pack and she gave me a little box. Inside was a ring, a real one with a blue stone.

"That's your birthstone. You have to be careful with it. When you wear it, think about your granny."

I slid it on my finger. I had a real ring. It was all mine.

Mama, Granny, Daddy, and me piled into the car. I still tried to figure out a way to keep Granny with us.

As we stood at the gate, waiting for Granny's plane, I had the best idea ever. The plane taxied into place.

Granny squatted in front of me. "Bye, Annie, you be a good girl. Be my special doll. I love you."

Loneliness and desperation washed over me. "Wait! Don't go. Please don't go."

Both Mama and Daddy laughed. How cute that I wanted Granny to stay.

"I have to go back to work so I can send you more toys. Your mama has promised to bring you down to visit me soon."

"No." I screamed the word. "I have an idea. Take me with you. I want to live with you. I promise to be good."

Again the laugh from Mama and Daddy. "You would want your mama as soon as it was time to go to bed," Daddy said.

I understood that if Granny walked away, Mama would go back to her old ways. "No. I wouldn't. I'll do good with Granny. Please let me go." I directed this to Mama.

Mama's face turned mad. "You don't want to live with me?"

"Of course she does," Granny twittered, like a little nervous bird to close to an enemy.

But I wanted to be away from Mama.

"I'll see you soon. I promise." She smiled.

In a whirlwind of hugs, Granny was gone, walking across the tarmac to the steps. When she reached the door, she turned and gave us a wave.

Everything eventually went back to normal after Granny left. But at first, Mama didn't sew for a week. Instead, she sat on the sofa and watched soap operas all day. For supper she cooked banana pudding and chocolate cake. Daddy teased that she would gain back the weight she lost if she didn't stop eating sweets, so she started sewing again and put a pot of chicken and dumplings on the stove. Her new project was my summer dresses, and I was forced to stand still while she tucked and pinned.

A couple of months after Granny left, someone knocked on the door one hot morning. Mama padded to answer it in her slippers.

A woman with bright orange hair wound up on her head stood there in shorts that exposed at least a million freckles.

"We just moved in two houses down," she said to Mama. "Your husband and mine work together. I need some coffee. I'm dying for a cup of coffee."

In our front yard were six kids of all sizes.

The woman looked at me. "Go out there and play with them. Your mama and me are going to talk and drink coffee."

I waited for Mama to say no.

"Stay in the yard, Ann." Mama seemed in shock.

I ran before she could change her mind. Playing in the front yard with kids was a dream come true. I even got dirty. The older three kids built a fort out of leftover bricks that were piled up on the side of the house. I crawled in after a girl my age and the wall crashed in on us, hitting me in the head. It hurt, but I didn't want to stop playing until I rubbed some blood from my head onto my hand.

"Don't scream," said the oldest boy. He was at least eight. "Our moms will come out and make us quit playing." He grabbed a handful of leaves off the tree and used them to wipe the blood away. "We got to put some water on your hair. It shows the blood because it's blond."

He took the water hose and sprayed my head. I wanted to scream because I didn't like water on my head, but I held the urge in until he finished.

"There, now it's gone."

My head stung, but playing was more important.

What seemed like hours later, Mama and the woman came out on the porch.

"You come to my house tomorrow morning, Jeanette."

Mama smiled. "I will. What time?"

"Lord, I get up at the crack of dawn. Anytime you want. I'll be there. You can help me decide on curtains."

"We will be there."

Mama stayed true to her word, and we went to the woman's house the next morning. I learned that her name was Molly. The kids came flooding out of the house to play. We ran and got dirty, building a tree house and playing freeze tag. I forgot how much I missed Granny.

A couple of weeks after Mama met Molly, Daddy came home from work a little early. He was holding something against him.

"What do you have?" I could see we weren't taking our usual scooter ride.

"It's a surprise." Daddy laughed.

Mama stood at the front door.

The bundle moved and I took a step back. "What is that?"

Daddy laughed again. "You have to come see."

I stepped forward. Daddy pulled away the brown towel, and I saw something black and white with lots of fur. "It's a puppy!" I reached out. "Look at his flappy ears."

"Let's take him in the backyard." Daddy walked through the house and out the kitchen door. I was close behind.

"We can't have a dog, Glover."

"Hush, Jeanette. Every kid deserves a dog of their own."

"You know she can't keep it. What will we do?"

"Hush now, let's enjoy this."

Mama was quiet.

Daddy put the dog on the ground, and it chased me, snapping at the back of my panties, tearing them. I giggled and ran some more. A puppy.

I named him Peppe and loved him best of all.

"Ann, we have to wash that hair," Mama called from bathroom.

I froze and wished all of my hair would fall out so I didn't have to wash it ever again.

"Now."

I stood in my room.

There was a knock on the front door. I peeked out and saw Molly standing on the front stoop.

"We can't go off until Ann gets her hair washed," Mama said to her. "That takes forever because she is afraid of the water."

"Kids, get out of the car and stay in the front yard," Molly yelled. "We will be ready to go in a minute." She walked in and spied me watching. "Come on, Ann. I know how to wash your hair, and you won't be afraid. I promise."

"She throws horrible fits. You can't stop that," Mama fussed.

Molly came into my room and picked up two cups from my tea set. "This is perfect. Come along, young lady."

I went. What choice did I have?

"Bring that high stool over here by the sink," Molly said to me, pointing at the stool that sat in the corner of the kitchen. Then she patted the seat. "Up here." She looked at Mama. "Shampoo and a towel."

Molly pushed on my shoulder. "You have to help me. Hold each teacup over an ear. I'm going to pour the water over your head. I promise not to get it in your eyes, and it can't get in your ears as long as you keep the cups in place."

I wanted to cry but I knew Mama would only force me to get in the tub. Molly guided my head back and began to pour warm water over my head. Not a bit went into my eyes or ears. I was through in no time.

"See." Molly dried my hair with the towel. "Now get ready. We're going for ice cream. Your mom and me have important stuff to talk about."

Weeks went by, and it was almost time for Molly's older kids to start school. "We're going to the PX to buy school supplies. Want to go?" she asked Mama.

"We can't. Glover is coming home early to take care of something." Mama gave Molly a look.

Molly frowned. "Let Ann go with us. She can do something fun."

"I don't know."

"It will be easier if she is with me."

Mama agreed, and I was over the moon.

We had so much fun in Molly's station wagon. The older

boys acted crazy, poking us girls in the ribs. Once, Molly pulled off the road and threatened to spank them. Everybody laughed because they knew she wouldn't spank anyone. She was a good mom and didn't have it in her. After shopping, we all got ice cream cones. Mine was chocolate, and I ate it so fast my head hurt.

Molly dropped me off at home, and I ran to the backyard to see Peppe. He didn't meet me on the stoop like he always did. "Peppe." Still no puppy.

Mama and Daddy came out.

"Where is Peppe?"

Mama looked at Daddy. "You tell her." She stomped into the house, slamming the screen door.

"Ann."

"Did someone take Peppe? He's gone."

"I took him." He squatted to my level.

"Why?" I tried my best not to cry in front of him. He hated tears.

"I had to take him to a new home." He placed his arm round me.

"Why?" I wailed.

"Listen now. Listen." He waited, quiet.

When I finished, he dried my eyes with the handkerchief he kept in his pocket. "We have to move and Peppe can't come. I took him to a place where he will find a new home."

"A new home. He's mine. Why can't he move with us?"

"Because we have move to another country. We can't take a dog to Germany. Your mother and you are leaving for your grandmother's next week. I will make sure our stuff is shipped, along with the car."

"You're not coming with us to Granny's?"

He shook his head and took the handkerchief back, folding it into a neat square. "No. I will go to Germany first. You and your mother will wait at your grandmother's. After Christmas, you will fly to Germany to live."

"You won't be there for Christmas?" The tears threatened again.

"No, but you have to be brave. You're a soldier's daughter. All this crying is for prissy pants."

This made me giggle.

"You have to be brave and help your mom. Can you do this? You'll be on a mission just like me."

I nodded.

He stood and slapped his leg. "Good. Stand at attention, Private Swafford."

I stood and saluted.

"And you get to ride on a train all the way to your grandmother's."

A train. I had always wanted to ride a train.

We said our goodbyes to Molly and her family. Molly made ice cream sundaes, and Mama ate a big one covered in chocolate syrup. Once when Mama thought I was not around, she sobbed. "How will I make it without you, Molly?"

I worried about this too. Since we met Molly, Mama hadn't given me one spanking.

Molly snapped her fingers. "You'll find another friend, Jeanette. Just like that. And that is an order." She hugged Mama, kissing the top of her head. Mama really loved Molly. Sometimes I thought she was happier with Molly than with Daddy. When we walked home, I took Mama's hand in mine. It was sweaty and hot.

"We will be happy. We have to be brave," Mama said.

She stopped briefly and looked down at me. The late August sun was beginning to make long fall shadows on the yards. A cool breeze sprinkled over my skin. Change was here.

We walked home hand in hand.

"Ann?"

"Yes, Mama?"

"If you want to call me 'Mother' like I call your granny, you can. It's what big girls do."

Mother.

"Ok."

Stone 24
The Train Ride

Mama and I boarded the train in Richmond, Virginia. Daddy watched us from the platform. We had suitcases, and the other items we needed to get us through our stay at Granny's were on the way in a box shipped from the post office the day before. "Our box will almost meet us." Mother sighed. The inside of the train is my one crystal-clear memory with vivid details from that day: the texture of the seats, the smells of different perfumes and men's cologne mixed together, the darkness of the passenger car, the cigarette smoke hanging above the heads of other riders.

For the life of me, I can't remember how long the actual trip took.* I don't recall sleeping, but surely I did. What comes to mind is my conversation with two nuns in full habit who were sitting near me. Actually, they allowed me to talk and talk and talk and talk. Never losing patience with me.

I don't remember looking out the train windows, but I must have. Mother would have pointed out some scenery, told me a story. Surely I played with the shades on the windows by pulling them up and down. We had to have eaten because the trip wouldn't have been a short one. I don't know. Those memories are gone.

---

* In 1960, trains were still being used frequently for travel. The routes were direct and the trip times much shorter than we have today. For more, see Tom Vanderbilt, "Stop This Train!" May 15, 2009, *Slate*, http://www.slate.com/articles/life/transport/2009/05/stop_this_train.html.

As we neared the train station in Atlanta, Mother called me to the windows across the aisle from us.[†] "Watch now. The train is going to enter the station. You may see your granny, but don't worry if you don't. She will be there."

I pressed my face against the window and watched as the train entered the covered area. Many people waited. I scanned their faces but not one woman looked familiar. Then I saw her. She was standing a little apart from everyone else, wearing a yellow dress belted at the waist. I put my hand to the window.

"Granny, Granny. I'm here, can you see me?" But the train zipped right by. I began to sob.

Mother tried to gather me in her arms, but I wouldn't let her. I howled like a wounded animal.

"It's okay. The train will stop and we will get off."

"But she can't find us in all those people," I sobbed.

"Oh, I have a feeling she heard you when we went by." Mother gave a quick laugh, looking at the other passengers.

The train did stop. Mother and I made our way to the door. The conductor tipped his hat and winked at me. I searched the people but didn't see Granny.

"She's not here. She's not here. We went too far." I tried to pull away from Mother and look on my own.

"She's here, and if you get away from me, you'll be lost. Do you want that?"

I relaxed and allowed her to guide me into the crowd. And

[†] The Atlanta Terminal Station was located on Spring Street and designed by P. Thornton Marye, also known for designing the Fox Theatre. The terminal was completed in 1905 and torn down in 1971. The Richard B. Russell Federal Building now stands in its place. See https://en.wikipedia.org/wiki/Terminal_Station_%28Atlanta%29.

before I even realized what had happened, Granny was standing in front of me.

"How is my doll?" Her sweet smile made up for her being lost from us.

"She has had a doozie of a trip," Mother said. She hugged Granny in a warm embrace. Maybe leaving Virginia wasn't going to be too bad. Up until this point, my life had been sheltered and involved a trip or two each week to the store. With the exception of Mother's new friend Molly, we never did anything much. To say I was in overload mode was an understatement.

We made our way through the crowd and into Granny's car, an old pea-green Plymouth, probably a 1948 or so. Nothing like our 1960 Plymouth Valiant that was almost the same color but had that wonderful new car smell. Granny's car smelled old, but I loved the soft squishy seats. I bounced and bounced. "Hey, don't pop a spring back there," she said, watching me in the rearview mirror. Granny drove us through the large city of Atlanta, much bigger and more modern than Richmond. Mother actually laughed a few times.

"So, tell me how long you two will be with me," Granny said to Mother.

"I know through the holidays. There isn't any base housing. Glover says Hahn is huge, but too many families. He has to find a good place for us in one of the villages. I don't know how long that will take."

"It's a long way. I can't imagine living in a German town. You can't even speak the language. How will you make it?" Granny looked at me in the mirror again. "I hope you stay with me a nice long time." She glanced back at Mother. "Have you talked to Ann about what she has to have done?"

"No, not yet, Mother."

"I think we should explain it to her. It happens next week," Granny said in a quiet voice.

"What happens?"

Mother looked back at me. "You are going in the hospital to have your tonsils out."

"Why?" A desperate feeling ran through my body.

"Because of all your sore throats. You know how you hate shots. Remember?"

Each time I went to the doctor, I got a shot of penicillin. My throat infections happened so often, Mother tried to find different routes to drive to the doctor's office so I wouldn't begin screaming. When I saw the building, I knew I was in for a needle.

"I don't have sore throats anymore." I said this in hopes of not having to go to the hospital.

"It's summer. You will start getting sick again soon. Having your tonsils removed will help a lot."

"And, you get ice cream and Jell-O. Lots of it," Granny added.

My tonsils were removed the next week. And just like Granny promised, I was allowed to eat ice cream and Jell-O as much as I wanted. The problem was that my throat hurt so bad I didn't want to eat or drink anything. Neither Granny nor Mother had told me about this part. But after a few hours, I was eating ice cream and feeling a little better.

Mother continued to be nice. I didn't get any spankings. Around Granny, just like when she was with Molly, Mother was calm and happy. Daddy's letters came regularly, and both of us got excited to read them. He was searching for an apartment in the small villages that surrounded the base.

Then Granny got an idea. "Why don't we enroll Annie in kindergarten at the Methodist Church?"

"I don't know. Ann isn't used to staying with anyone, and I don't want her getting sick. All those kids will have germs," Mother answered.

"But she could play with the kids and learn something too." Granny winked at me.

In late 1960, kids didn't have to go to kindergarten, so Mother was quite satisfied to keep me home.

"She can't go the whole year," Mother said.

"That doesn't matter. She will still have some learning time." Granny was and always would be an advocate for education.

"I don't think I should spend the money," Mother countered.

"I'll pay for it," Granny offered.

What could Mother say to that?

Kindergarten was the first place where I discovered I wasn't like all the other kids. I didn't want to please the teachers. I wanted to go home. I told my teachers I hated the room, the books, puzzles, and the games. Kids know when grownups don't like them. Soon I was pulled away from the other children to put puzzles together with one of the teachers rather than play with the groups. The reason this happened wasn't and still isn't clear to me. My dresses were the best. My hair was always clean and tangle free. My shoes were shiny black patent. So it had to be what I said or how I played. I'm not sure, but I was separated. And I hated school.

Halfway through each morning, the class would assemble in perfect lines and march down the hall, down a flight of stairs, and into the kitchen of the church, where we were each given a glass bottle of chocolate milk—all milk was packaged in glass at that time. I loved chocolate and treasured the fact that I was allowed to have an ice-cold bottle all to myself. We had to carry our bottles back the same route to our room. One morning, somehow, my sweaty bottle slid from my hands onto the stairs and shattered into a million pieces, not to mention spraying milk all over everything within twenty feet of me.

"Get over here, Ann." The teacher's voice was mean. "You will not have another bottle of milk. You were a bad girl."

And I didn't receive a snack either. I watched from my lonely table as the other children ate their cookies and drank their milk.

When Mother picked me up at lunchtime, I broke into sobs as we left the school. She parked the car and took me inside to get to the bottom of my tears.

"Excuse me," Mother said as she stood in front of the teacher. "Why is Ann so upset?"

"She was punished today for dropping her bottle of chocolate milk on the stairs. It got all over her, the stairs, the walls, and other children."

"So you didn't give her a milk?"

The teacher frowned. "She didn't get milk or a snack. I have to tell you, we moved her to a table by herself. She is a bad influence on the other children. She talks smart to us." The teacher had her hand on her hip.

Mother took my hand. "Well, you think I don't know what this is about. You think I don't know you. Ann will not be back at this horrible school. And you will refund all the money we paid." She pulled me out of the building. I was sure she would spank me, but Mother walked as straight and tall as she could as we crossed the parking lot. When we were safely in the car, she frowned at me.

"That woman calls herself a teacher. I went to high school with her. She has a problem with the way I walk. Always did. Made fun of me. I'm sorry you were mistreated because of me. I hate being back in this place. It's not good for us to live here. We just have to make it through Christmas."

This was the first time I understood that Mother's wobbly walk wasn't what others thought of as normal. That some in her hometown rejected her, that she thought she was second best or worse, and that maybe these feelings were a legacy passed on to me.

Stone 25
Bridges Falling Apart

We stepped off the plane in Frankfurt, Germany, while hard snow rained down, covering the runway and rapidly collecting on the steps rolled in front of the plane's door. Fat snowflakes settled on my dark blue wool coat before they disappeared. They caught in Mother's eyelashes. She pointed to the tarmac. Daddy stood behind the ribbon barrier, grinning his gapped-tooth smile.

"Daddy, it's snowing," I yelled to him.

All the passengers behind and in front of us laughed.

"We're from Georgia," Mother explained.

Daddy scooped me into one of his arms and used the other to hold Mother close. "I'm so glad to see my girls," he said.

After picking up our suitcases at baggage claim, Daddy escorted us to our car that had beat us over the ocean by a month. "Did you miss our lady?" This was his name for the green Plymouth Valiant he treasured.

I nodded and crawled in the backseat.

The car trip seemed to go on forever, so I listened to my parents talk.

"You will like the apartment in the village. You can't imagine what the place is like, Jeanette."

Mother chewed her bottom lip. "I hope I can get used to all these changes."

Outside the car window, the city disappeared and the road looped through the valley. To our right was a wide river.

"That's called the Rhine River," Daddy said, pointing.

The mountains were around us, and on top of one were the ruins of a castle. "Look," I shouted. "Did a king and queen live there?"

"Probably, but in Germany you call them emperor and empress."

The landscape was covered in a thick white blanket that softened the river and turned the place into a fairy tale. The road climbed into the mountains with plenty of curves. Eventually, we came into the village of Hahn, and I stared out the window at the store fronts and snow-covered streets. To our left was a large church-like building, but part of the roof was round, with no steeple like the churches at home—only a small cross. A wagon pulled by large horses clopped in front of us. There were no cars except ours. Finally, Daddy pulled over in front of a two-story stucco building with a stone wall around its backyard. A boy around my age was skating, ice skating, on the road in front of the house.

"You can talk to him." Mother nudged me.

I slid on the ice, almost falling. "My name is Ann. I live here now. I came from America. My daddy is a soldier."

The boy stopped skating and gave me an odd look. Then he began to speak, but I couldn't understand a word he was saying. I burst into tears, which drove the boy away. Daddy took my hand and led me to the front yard of the house. "He was speaking German. You can't understand him now. But one day you will. You will learn to speak German too."

We followed Daddy around the side of the house and through the wooden gate in the wall. A set of stairs climbed up the back of the house to a platform. We took each step carefully. "Carl cleaned the snow from the steps, but it's been snowy since this morning. You can't keep anything cleared."

"Who is Carl?" Mother asked.

"He and Gertrude own the house."

At the top was a wooden door. Daddy inserted a skeleton key into its lock, and we went into our small apartment.

"Oh my, the living room is tiny." Mother put her hands on her hips and stood in the middle of the room. It didn't feel so small to me because there was only a chaise lounge and a small desk against the wall, which was so thick the windowsill became a seat that looked over the backyard. The kitchen was tiny compared to the one we had in Virginia, but it was big enough for a small table with three chairs, two matching and one odd. There was a bathroom with a clawfoot tub and a bedroom with two twin beds pushed together. A large wardrobe stood at the foot of the beds against the wall. There was no bedroom for me. This pleased me beyond all reason. Now I didn't have to worry about sleeping alone. I had no choice but to sleep with my parents.

And that is what I got for thinking.

"We will make you a bed on the lounge in the living room," Daddy said with a smile.

I so wanted to please him. I hadn't seen him for months. I needed to be his good girl. I went to sit on the chaise knowing there was no way and nohow I could sleep in that creepy living room alone. But Daddy expected me to do just that.

That night I went to bed like my parents wanted. I had a warm blanket and a soft pillow. My favorite Barbie was on my chest. I told myself stories after Daddy finished reading to me from the Bible. The door to my parents' bedroom was shut and the night was black. Blacker than I could ever remember a room. I covered my face with the blanket but then I couldn't breathe. I strained to listen. Were my parents still awake? All buildings have creaks and groans, but this one was an old, old house. I knew it had to be. And it was probably full of ghosts or monsters. I don't know how long I stayed on the chaise before I decided to make my way to my parents' bedroom. Those beds pushed together made one big bed. Maybe I could lie on the end and neither of them would notice.

I curled next to my daddy's legs. The room was so dark I couldn't see my hand in front of my face, but his scent and his hard muscles gave him away. I drifted off to sleep near the person I thought I could count on the most.

We spent eight months in the village, and I grew to love it. As a child I took a lot for granted. One late spring day, Mother took me to her friend's apartment with a window overlooking a parking lot in the middle of town. We—the friends, her daughter, Mother, and me—stood watching and waiting. A wagon processional moved down the road toward the parking lot. In the wagon sitting high, so that everyone could see, was a bald man wearing all white. Kids and parents followed behind with arms of flowers.

Mother whispered in my ear, "This is history, Ann. Something you will remember the rest of your life. You will tell your kids about it."

The pope had come to visit the small village of Hahn. I fell in love with the tons of flowers thrown at this man who was held in such high esteem. After he prayed in a language I didn't know—I think Italian—the wagon pulled away, and I went into the stone paved streets and gathered all the beautiful flowers my small arms could hold. Mother helped me. We smiled and laughed together.

Our years in Germany were probably the most normal in my life. Mother made friends and Daddy seemed to enjoy his family. Chicken and dumplings disappeared from the dinner menu. Mother smiled more, and I started school.

Christmas in base housing turned out to be magical, even in the midst of Cold War Germany. Hahn Air Force Base was located a mere sixty miles from the Berlin Wall. My mother must have been terrified of this fact, but she never showed the emotion. Daddy worked on classified projects that involved missiles stored deep in the ground.*

Children are resilient, and I gave little thought to the weapons in silos and bunkers. The world outside my bedroom window was a fairy-tale forest full of gypsies and wild boars. The thought of both sent thrills across my scalp. If a family photo existed from this time in my life, the picture would be black and white, crinkled around the edges. Mother would wear a plain dress, belted at the waist, her hair already turning white at the age of thirty-four. I would be dressed in my glorious red, green, and black plaid jumper made by Mother for the Christmas season. Daddy, standing behind us solid and dependable, dressed in his military fatigues, would have a stern look on his face, his soldier face. But, at the last minute, just as the camera clicked, a half smile would appear, revealing a space between his front teeth that would later show up in two of my daughters.

That first year we lived on base, a week before Christmas Eve, Daddy huffed around, waiting on me to don rubber snow

* Hahn Air Force Base was the frontline NATO facility in Germany for over forty years of the Cold War. In 1959, all American atomic weapons were moved from French soil to Hahn, where they would remain for years. For more, see "Hahn Air Force Base," https://ipfs.io/ipfs/QmXoypizjW3WknFiJnKLwHCnL72vedxjQkDDP1mXWo6uco/wiki/Hahn_Air_Base.html.

boots and layers of clothes and gloves. We tramped out of the apartment into the snow, deep enough to slide inside the tops of my boots.

I looked around, sniffing the air. "I smell icicles."

"There is no such odor, Ann," Daddy grumbled.

But I detected the clean, faintly sweet fragrance that only icicles could give. I never uttered one complaint about my cold feet, even as my toes went to tingling.

Our mission: search out the perfect tree and bring it home.

Daddy, being a soldier, worked at all tasks with the same dogged determination he must have used when marching to the front in World War II—maybe right where we stood. After all, he had been part of the liberation troops that set the prisoners free from the concentration camps less than twenty years before.

The forest was dense, but bright due to the snow that coated everything with pure light. I imagined that the ice crystals falling from the higher branches of the trees were fairies dancing to music of their own. I joined them, a ballerina twirling and leaping until Daddy turned and glared at me.

"Quiet." He spoke in a loud whisper as he pointed ahead.

The tree, the best tree ever, sat in a clearing as if the other trees had stepped back to give her—I knew it was a female tree—room to grow round and full, thick with short needles. She was shorter than all the other trees, which only made her more appealing, especially to a Christmas tree hunter like my daddy.

I pointed to the branches where the snow had settled in clumps. "Can't we take her home just like this?"

Daddy made the sound he always made over my silly ideas. He mumbled under his breath as he circled the tree, leaving large footprints in the snow. I followed, placing my boots into each print. When he stopped I ran into his back.

He turned with a frown. "Careful."

In one hand was the bow saw. He studied his prize with serious concentration, like a master builder about to choose his first cut. After much chin rubbing and muttering, he squatted for a long look. An eternity went by before he cut into the tree's trunk.

I heard a sigh of pain, a sadness released into the air.

When I told him this, he shook his head. "Ann," he said sternly, "you have your head full of dreams." His voice was soft and firm at the same time. He made a clean cut through the trunk, sawing with a speed that caused tiny pieces of wood to fly. I turned my face away and thought instead of the strands of lights and strings of popcorn I would lace through the branches.

In great detail, I described the decorations I would hang on this special tree and the red-haired angel with golden wings that I would place at the top. "She protects us," I explained.

This comment brought a half smile that smoothed the lines around Daddy's mouth. He trudged off, his combat boots leaving tracks at the attack scene. The tree was pulled behind him, clearing a path through the forest that I felt privileged to step into.

As we continued on our mission, each tree became a hiding place for the enemy, and I instructed Daddy to keep low so their fire wouldn't hit us or damage our prize, our prisoner, the perfect Christmas tree. We snaked our way through the woods, one careful step at a time, back into the bright daylight of another world, our world, if only for a while.

We tugged the tree, fingers touching, through the snow,

past the silent, deserted playground, now covered with a blanket of white. The sun rode the sky with little warmth, but still the icicles began to fade, one drip at a time. My feet had gone numb long before the business of dragging the tree. We left our prize by the front door and entered the warm, steamy house, the aroma of banana bread reminding me how normal Mother acted now. She looked up from a ball of cookie dough she was rolling. Cutout sugar cookies. Little bowls of green, red, and white sugar sprinkles sat around.

When I caught a smile Daddy exchanged with Mother, I knew this was a rare time, a scene that wouldn't last, and I should hold on to its flimsy tails as long as I could.

While we lived on the base there was no physical abuse, no use of the belt as discipline. And by the time I began second grade, Mother had loosened her hold. I was allowed to roam with the other kids in the thick forest that surrounded the housing on base, play hide and seek in the attics that I no longer feared, and ride my bike without the baby training wheels. We had a real life with friends who visited for dinner and holidays, friends Mother had coffee with after Daddy left for work. Normal.

Mother had a maid who came to clean on Fridays. Her name was Gertrude. She was young and beautiful with long dark hair and gold earrings that hung from a hole in each ear. Gertrude was a shared maid. Four friends of Mother would chip in for Gertrude to spend the week at a different apartment cleaning and cooking. She slept in a maid's room in the basement of our building. Since she worked at our house every Friday, Mother's job was to drop Gertrude at the bus stop in the village of Hahn after she finished our home. The last time I saw Gertrude, she sat at our little table in the kitchen eating toast with peanut butter and sugar. Mother and I laughed and talked with her. She had an infectious personality that pulled both of us into its glow. Mother left me with a friend and climbed into our Plymouth Valiant to take Gertrude to the bus. Just as she went to sit in the passenger side, she waved at me with a smile. That's what I remember of this girl, who couldn't have been any older than eighteen.

When Gertrude didn't show up at the bus stop on Monday, no one worried too much. The women thought she might be sick. When no one had heard from Gertrude by Wednesday, the women began to worry. Surely she would send word. She was such a punctual employee. A week went by before a police investigator from the village where Gertrude lived came to see the families. They wanted to speak with Mother most because it seems she was the last person to see Gertrude alive, standing at the bus stop with her suitcase in her hand. A few days later she was found in the Rhine River, wearing every piece of clothing that had been in her suitcase, probably in hopes she would sink. She had been strangled with a piece of cord that remained around her neck.

Mother reported to the investigator that Gertrude had been talking to a tall, handsome young man when she left her to wait on the bus. I never heard whether the killer was caught or not.

Germany wove good and bad memories into my fabric. After my brother Jeff was born, things began to go downhill in our family. Daddy spent more time away from home in the evenings. There was impatience in his voice when he spoke to Mother. He hardly held Jeff. Yet photos exist showing the opposite of these memories: Daddy stretched on a blanket outside, me just behind him and Jeff lying beside him. He is smiling a wide smile, as if being a father to his children is all he ever wanted.

Around the time Jeff was six months old, Daddy took me to the only toy store on the base. The large building was filled with toys of every kind. After living on base for at least two years, this was my first visit. Daddy was buying me a Skipper doll, Barbie's younger sister. There I stood looking at the blond and brunette Skippers. Which one? I chose the brunette to match my own hair, which had changed from blond, even though deep down I wanted the blond. Daddy bought Jeff a rubber football. He was six months old. There weren't many choices for that age in 1964. With our purchases made, we set off for home.

Mother frowned when I showed her my doll. She wasn't frowning at me. She wasn't even looking at me. Instead, she looked at the rubber football with the inked-in price of sixty cents. "You bought him a rubber ball, Glover? Ann's doll cost eight dollars. You only spent sixty cents on your son?"

A fight cranked out with her words and ended with Daddy stomping out.

Mother turned to me. "You should throw that doll away. A good sister would do that."

I was six and wanted that doll, much more than a fussy baby brother. My silence said it all.

Mother glared at me with pure hate and disgust. This was the day things changed for the worse between Mother and me.

There is a black-and-white photo of Mother holding me the day she brought me home from the hospital. She is wearing a bewildered look, as if she would keep me at arm's length for the rest of my life, and that is basically what she did. In my mind, from the moment I chose the doll over Jeff, she put him first. In all likelihood, her favor for Jeff began when he was born.

In the middle of this turmoil between my parents, we took a trip to Cologne, Germany, to see the beautiful grand gothic cathedral. Dad was driving and I sat next to him as we crossed the long Hohenzollern suspension bridge across the Rhine River.[†]

"This bridge was blown up at the end of the war by the retreating German troops. Those on the bridge went into the Rhine and died." Daddy said this to Mother, who was sitting in the backseat breastfeeding Jeff.

With these words, fear engulfed me, unreasonable terror that would haunt me as an adult. I worried that the bridge would explode under us, killing us all or, worse, killing everyone but me. I would be left alone. To this day, I have a recurring nightmare of me attempting to cross a bridge. Halfway over the structure it begins to fall apart, and I am left trying to find the most stable place to ride down as the structure collapses.

That little girl, me, wanted to save her family. She couldn't. Daddy would find many women more satisfying then

---

[†] In Roman times the Rhine River was the northeastern border of the Roman Empire. The first bridge to cross the Rhine in Cologne was built around AD 310. Some of the ancient foundation of this original bridge is on display in the Romisch-Germanisches Museum. In 1945, at the end of World War II, the retreating German Army blew up all the bridges crossing the Rhine. The Hohenzollern Bridge was one of them. Only three years later, the bridge was repaired and put into use. In 1959, the Hohenzollern Bridge was completely reconstructed, and the intimating entrances were torn down and never replaced. See "Hohenzollern Bridge," *A View on Cities*, http://www.aviewoncities.com/cologne/hohenzollernbrucke.htm.

Mother. Maybe he always had. He would abandon us with Granny and not reappear in my life—with the exception of one disastrous visit—until I was sixteen, when I found him by calling an operator in a phone booth on the side of the road.

Stone 26
Haint on the Porch

After Daddy left us at Granny's for good, he went to his assignment in Savannah, Georgia, and life turned dark and dull. I hated most Sundays. Almost every week the day came wrapped the same way. Granny stretched out on the tan sofa in the tiny living room, cluttered with Mother's pieces shipped there from Germany. An oversized, framed oil painting hung on the wall over a chair and ottoman known as Arthur's chair because he sat in it each time he visited. When I sat down, it was in the swivel rocker so I could rock. This soothed me, as it still does when I am stressed. In one of my many therapy sessions, the doctor said I rock because Mother didn't nurture me enough when I was a baby or as a young child.

The curtains were closed tight throughout Granny's house. Only the window above the sofa was open to the natural light. Other kids from school had big dinners on the table after church. In our house, Mother was in bed, the room darkened as if it were night. She had no use for church or family dinners. But once a month, sometimes twice if we were lucky, we went to visit Granny's family on Holcomb Bridge Road just outside of Roswell. We always visited Aunt Stella—Granny's younger sister—at her rundown house that was lifted off the ground by tall towers of field stones on each corner and under the big front porch. My cousins and I could crawl beneath the house from the front yard to the back, and we did so often when we went out to play. Stella was a Fouts because she married Corine's cousin, Dugone. This wasn't his real name, but I only knew him as Uncle Dugone. When I first met him after coming back to Georgia, he sat on the wide front porch, wearing his work uniform smeared with black grease. His fingernails were caked with black. "He's a mechanic, Annie. He works on cars all day. His fingers are stained, not dirty," Granny explained. "He works in Roswell and makes really good money."

But I saw them as nasty. Dugone and Stella's house sure didn't look like they had money. And, when Dugone smiled at me, I saw he didn't have many teeth. Of course I stared.

But this didn't hurt his feelings at all. He only laughed at me. "I have to eat my food just like a baby does. All runny and slimy." He looked very serious.

My heart broke for a man who had to eat like a baby, and I made a silent promise to brush my teeth better.

He laughed again, then pulled a pouch of something out of his pocket and rolled it into a paper. When he finished, it looked like one of Daddy's cigarettes, but messier. He lit it with a shiny Zippo lighter—the kind Daddy used to add lighter fluid to once a week or so. "I'm pulling your leg, girl." Dugone laughed again and drew on the cigarette.

"Be careful, Dugone. She's not used to your mess." Granny gave him one of her half smiles.

"Lord, woman, you ain't changed a bit. Not one. Never will and I say that's a good thing, no matter what that there brother of yours says. He's a pain in the rear. And he don't approve of me either."

Granny nodded toward me. "Don't color the child's opinions of Ernest just yet. She hasn't met him."

Uncle Dugone shook his head. "I have some good whiskey under the sink. You want a taste?"

Now, I was shocked. For the whole seven months we'd

been at Granny's house, she never drank a drop of anything except sweet tea, ice water, and milk. She did have a cup of black coffee each morning before work, always sipping out of delicate china cups with gold inlaid rims and handles.

"I don't do that." Granny's voice sounded mad.

"You, not drink. Now there's a big fib. At your age, drinking don't matter so much anymore."

Granny was fifty-eight at the time, younger than I am now by two years. But she was ageless. Always the same. Old was Mother with her premature solid silver hair that she refused to do anything with other than keep it cut very short. She kept my hair in a pixie cut as well. My whole childhood, I yearned for long hair that touched my shoulders, but Mother wouldn't have it. Short hair was easier to wash and comb.

"I'm going in to see my sister." Granny opened the creaky screen door.

"Well, talk some sense into her. She's done got mad at me again. Says I'm not taking care of myself. Hell, what am I doing that I didn't do thirty years ago?"

Granny frowned. "Don't say such words around Annie."

"And it's Sunday too. Lord, Inas, I ain't never known you to be a Jesus person."

Granny flinched. "We all have our ways of honoring the Lord."

"Yeah, that's what I say, Inas. Go on in there. That woman done made one of her orange cakes from scratch. Just for Jeanette. How's she doing anyway?"

Mother had stayed home with Jeff to take a nap. She really liked to take naps when she wasn't working at the Gas Light Company.

"She's fair to middling." Granny looked sad.

"She thought a lot of her husband. That's what Stellar said. I don't understand men now. I ain't been the best husband, and the whole town knows that, but I was always here for my kids. Might have been drunk as a skunk but I was here."

"Things are not like they were." Granny motioned me into the front room with high ceilings. The space was cool and dark. The wooden floors were covered with a big rose-pattern rug. In the middle of the room was an iron woodstove like something out of a Laura Ingalls Wilder book—my favorite ones to read at the time. Soon enough the room became noisy with Aunt Stella and her daughter Doddie, whose name was pronounced with a long "o." Aunt Corine came next with several of her daughters because their mother couldn't drive. There were third cousins, loud and whiny boys who were promptly kicked outside to play. The offer for me to join them was given, but I turned them down. Later I would come to enjoy their adventurous energy and spirit. But that day I sat in the corner of the sitting room near a large potted plant, becoming still and invisible. In her own element, Granny turned into a woman I wouldn't have known had I not recognized her face. She talked in a slang that would have caused her to grab her heart if I had spoken like that. To my complete horror, she took the offer of a brown powder inside a small tin—snuff. She tucked it into her bottom lip. There was a shiny brass spittoon between Aunt Stella, Aunt Corine, and Granny where they spit the brown liquid. I thought I'd die, but I was thankful that Mother wasn't there to see her mother acting in such a way. There were greetings and catching up, all rather normal, but then I caught the word "haint."

"I seen Mama when I was five," Aunt Stella said. "She was

standing over my bed. It was before the big fire. She was watching over me."

I knew they were talking about Asalee, my great-grandmother. But when I did the math, I knew Aunt Stella would have been two and half when her mother died. I was the type of child who loved a story, but especially a spooky story. A chill walked across the part in my hair.

Granny clicked her tongue. "I never saw her looking after me. She was a good woman, too good."

How could a person be too good? Granny had told me the story of the day her mama died. I waited to see if she would tell it again. I never tired of hearing it.

But Stella wondered aloud if maybe Asalee came to her because of the way she died, how she was killed by Henry Lee. This was intriguing to me. I remained silent, knowing one noise would remind them I was in the room, and the real stories would be packed away.

At the feet of these women, I received an education on how to become a writer, a storyteller. I never got bored. When we left that afternoon—after eating large slabs of orange cake—I settled into the car. I needed to go to the bathroom something terrible, but Aunt Stella didn't have one. "Out back in the woods" was what she called the outhouse—a wooden bench with two holes, flies and bees buzzing around. No matter how bad I needed to relieve myself, I couldn't go into that place. I couldn't. Dying would have been easier.

Uncle Dugone waved from the porch as he smoked a homemade cigarette and drank something—I was sure it wasn't coffee—from an old mug.

I waved back. I wouldn't see him alive again. But I would see him—a month after his death—sitting in his chair on the porch, staring out into the forest across the street. He never acknowledged me, but this was the first time I saw a haint for myself.

Many people would report seeing Uncle Dugone there in his chair over the years. Now there is a neighborhood of houses where Aunt Stella lived. Did others see Uncle Dugone? Did he spend his time on the porch even though his house was gone and a large, beautiful new one stood in its place? It might be a question to ask the owners.

Stone 27
Hide and Seek

I never understood why Mother always went back to the little house on Joyner Avenue. Granny's house. No matter where life led her, she found her way back like a homing pigeon searching out her roost, her safe place. So we stayed on in the tiny house after Mother got a good job. Maybe she needed Granny to lead her, help her control her actions. My presence became a problem to Mother. Neither woman knew what to do with me since they both worked all day. Jeff was easy. He was three and went to nursery school. After school I was sent to an array of babysitters. One such caretaker, Mrs. Turner—old, bent over, and soft spoken but strong enough to lift her husband, who was debilitated by a severe stroke—didn't like to feed me. Her husband, his mouth hanging open to the side, propped in his hospital bed, moaned the whole time I was there. My presence seemed to either excite him or pain him. I could never tell. My hunger after school was epic. Mrs. Turner made me half a sandwich and a cup of water. If I asked to have more, she only shook her head. "A child doesn't need any more food until she goes home to eat." So I starved. I stayed there the longest, going after school every day for two months. Then, one day when Mother picked me up, Mrs. Turner told her that I troubled her sick husband too much.

Mother asked our neighbors in the house behind us. The Youngs were made up of the mother, Mrs. Young, who was tall, pretty, had a funny personality; Mr. Young, whom I didn't see much; and two grown sons still at home—Jack, a funny, good-looking man in his early twenties, and David Jr., a slightly older young man with a stern frown who worked at Lockheed Martin. In one corner of his large room was a desk where David Jr. drew planes from all angles. Mrs. Young swore that he really was a nice person, but I only saw a man mad at the world and all the people in it, especially kids. It was in the big living room of Mrs. Young that I watched the fight for civil rights unfold on the twenty-five-inch black-and-white TV. Riots. Groups of black people being sprayed with fire hoses. Police beating young men over the head with sticks. The scenes scared me. Mrs. Young assured me I had nothing to worry about because we didn't have any blacks in our neighborhood. No one would tolerate that. In my whole school, there were only two black students.

I was made fun of unmercifully because I could speak another language, German. The kids called me a Nazi, even when I explained my father was a solider in World War II and Korea. And it didn't help my cause that my father was gone, MIA. Mother was about to be divorced. Every day, she prepared me in case I was called into court, drilling me to say I did not want to live with my father. He was threatening to take me from Mother. She spent long afternoons in a lawyer's office, me in the car alone with the windows rolled up and doors locked. Thank goodness the weather was cool.

I was the problem child. I was the kid they didn't know how to contain. Jeff, on the other hand, was too young to form an opinion, to say he wanted to be with his father. To tell his nursery school that he saw a word, F-U-C-K, spray painted on the brick wall of the building across from the lawyer's office. I actually announced this at Mrs. Young's dinner table one evening when Mother was running late. Jack, the nice son, busted out laughing, while Mr. Young and David Jr' s faces turned bright red and their frowns grew more defined. Not long after this, Mrs. Young told Granny she couldn't keep me. Young ladies didn't even spell these kinds of words. The truth was I had no idea what the word meant, only that Mother said to forget I had seen it.

I begged to stay alone. "I'm old enough."

"There will be strict rules," Granny said. "No opening the door once you get home. No answering the phone unless it rings twice, stops, and rings again. This will be the code for you to answer. No cooking. You can only eat food from the pantry and the refrigerator. You have to do your homework. Stay away from the windows. Never tell anyone at school you're staying alone, even the teacher. Agreed?" She watched me, waiting.

"Yes ma'am." I was free. Amen. Free.

Then Daddy showed up.

It was a Saturday in early spring but it felt like summer. The divorce court date was coming up in early June. Mother warned me a few minutes before Daddy and his sisters, my aunts, arrived. As the car turned into the driveway, my heart felt like it might explode. I couldn't be there when he came in. I couldn't see him. If I did, Mother would know how I loved him more than her, and I would know how much I had failed as his daughter. I ran out the back door and around the back of the house and hid in a lilac bush that had leafed out early. I really believed he wouldn't come to look for me. The chain on the new storm door rattled and heavy footfalls sounded on the wooden stairs. After a minute, I saw his shiny loafers standing by the bush.

"Ann, come out."

Dying would have been much easier than stepping out of that bush. For a ten-year-old, a lifetime had passed since the last time I saw him. He had missed my birthday, Christmas, New Year's, and Easter without even a phone call. I didn't know him anymore, and I wasn't sure I wanted to know him.

I stepped out and there was Daddy, looking the same. Mother had gained weight and allowed her white hair to grow out of the blond color. If anything, Daddy was more handsome.

"Why are you hiding from me?" I heard all my own sadness in his voice. The sound took away my breath and my mind raced. In that moment, I understood that what had happened to our family was my fault. If not for me, maybe he would still be with Mother. I'm the one who told. I told about the other woman. Me. I wanted the new doll. I talked too much and needed too much attention. I was no help.

I stood still.

"You don't have to hide from me. What did your mother tell you about me?"

What was there to tell? Had she talked to him and I didn't know? And honestly he was the one who left us, abandoned us. He had been mad at me. "She hasn't told me anything. You haven't been here." My tone was sharp.

He looked at the ground. His clothes were wrinkle free, and the crease in his pants was perfect. His hair was a tad longer but not much. "Do you want to come inside? I brought Jeff and you something."

I shrugged. "Sure." But the tone of my voice was anything but sure.

I remember three things about this one and only visit

Daddy made to see me as a child. The first was Granny's face as she sat on the sofa. I'd been with her long enough to know when she was angry, even if the others in the room weren't aware. And maybe anger wasn't even the correct word for the vibes I felt soaking the air, radiating from Granny. Rage was probably the best description I could give. Mother sat in Arthur's chair with her feet on the stool. Her hair was longer than usual, unkept for her. Jeff played on the floor nearby. He could barely speak. The doctor had just told Mother he was tongue-tied and needed to have his tongue clipped soon. The thought of this procedure sent chills up my back. I'm ashamed to say I was really glad it wasn't me.

Two of Daddy's sisters, Mary and Lorine—one big and round, the other small and petite—sat on the sofa with Granny. Both wore a sore look on their faces as if they were in the presence of something very unpleasant. Was it Granny? Or me? Mother probably. Lately she had a sharp edge to her that flashed out at people when they were least expecting it. Most recently she went to use her Sears credit card and was told she no longer had credit because she was getting a divorce. Daddy had called all the companies of their shared cards and informed them. Mother did have a bad habit of running up debt, especially when she was depressed, so even Granny couldn't argue with his reasoning.

When Daddy and I walked into Granny's tiny living room that day, Mother looked at me. Her gaze was glassy, almost crazed.

"I told you she didn't want to see you, Glover." Mother's words curled around Daddy and squeezed, releasing their deadly venom.

Daddy ignored her, but his sisters took a deep breath in

unison.

"The both of you need to be careful with the kids' feelings," Granny said to Daddy.

He didn't look at her. Instead, he produced two packages wrapped in Christmas paper. Mine was taller than Jeff's square one. For the life of me, I cannot recall what Jeff received, but when I tore the paper from mine, a deep, deep, deep disappointment washed through me. As I removed the paper, I thought at first that Daddy had redeemed himself for running off and sending Mother divorce papers. A gift bought by him for me. Mother had told me numerous times that he didn't even acknowledge my past birthday and Christmas. She always rubbed this information into the wounds still fresh from their split.

I wanted to stop unwrapping the present, stop time, freeze it right there in that moment, stop everyone and everything from moving forward. Stop!

The room was deadly quiet. All attention was on me.

"Finish opening it, Ann." Mother's voice was ragged as if her words had caught on a sharp nail and torn apart.

"Give her a minute, Jeanette." This was not Daddy's voice, but Granny's.

Silly baby tears filled my chest and clogged my throat like English green peas used to do when I was forced to eat them. I could not cry in front of these people, who called me their family, waiting to use me as a weapon to finishing ripping the world apart. I swallowed, and the horrible pain backed off. The paper gathered around the gift when I finished.

"Glover, don't you know she's too old for a toy vacuum cleaner?" Mother said, jumping ahead of me. "We bought her one of those when she was three in Virginia. She can't play with that thing. You should have given her the money. Let her choose something she likes."

Part of me was thankful that she said this. The other part ached for my daddy. His disappointment and sadness rode the air. Couldn't anyone feel the heavy emotions hanging in the room?

"I can take it back." Daddy reached in his pocket and pulled out his wallet. "I'll give you some money." He stood there in that living room, ill fit for the dainty female decorations.

"No." I pulled the vacuum away from the paper. "I like it. I like it a lot."

Mother groaned and rolled her eyes.

Granny frowned.

Daddy broke into a grin. "I thought you might."

"I do. It looks like a real vacuum." I plugged it into the wall. This miniature Kenmore, complete with a light, actually did pick up debris. I pushed with a frantic need to please Daddy, to make him love me even if Mother would punish me in some way later.

The adults began to talk. I ran the vacuum. They talked with rising and falling crescendos, laced with grownup decisions and opinions. Mother began to cry silent tears. The small Kenmore moved fast across the thin green rug, blurring their voices with its tiny rumble. The rug was Mother's newest choice for Granny's house. Only the week before, I had come home from school to find our bedroom painted stomach medicine pink. Everything: molding, pegboard, shelves on the pegboard, windows. Pink, a color I never knew Mother liked. Granny had pinched her mouth together as if she were sucking on lemons, but she never complained. She looked the same way now, sitting on the sofa and taking in all the voices sounding off at once.

"Turn that thing off, Ann." Her words weren't mean. They were patient and exhausted.

The room fell silent except for the rumbling of the small engine. I turned the switch off. My knees went weak, and I sat on the floor with a plop.

"The visit is over for today." Granny stood.

Mother was sobbing.

My aunts were red in the face. Mary took a breath. "You can't decide when Glover can see his children."

Granny straightened her shoulders in a rigd line. "This is my house, not Glover's." She gave Mother, Jeff, and me a long look. "I think this little family has had quite enough. You can't come waltzing in here after months of not talking to them and expect everything to be like it was. What you did is not okay. You ran off and left them. As far as I'm concerned, you gave up your rights to these kids, but I don't decide this. A judge will be the one who decides when the divorce goes through."

Mother said the word "divorce" at least ten times a day, but hearing it from Granny's mouth made the whole situation real. Still, I didn't cry. I sat there and watched Mother cry. I thought she was weak, useless to save me. I thought the only way to be strong was to hold in the tears. I thought she was asking for trouble if she showed Daddy her feelings. Where did these thoughts come from?

When Daddy and my aunts left that day, I knew I wouldn't see any of them for a long time. And I was right: seven years would go by before I saw Daddy again. I would be a grown woman, pregnant with my second child, when I saw my aunts again. The Swafford family would not seek me out. Any contact between them and me was squashed that fateful day. But I was making friends, getting to know my great-aunts, and watching the world stretch out before me. Every kid loves summer, and I was no different. I deserved a good one. I prayed that the upcoming summer would be the best in my whole life. If only I had owned a crystal ball to stare into and see a warning of what was to come.

Stone 28
The Klan

If I thought my childhood had turned inside out with Dad's leaving, the summer of 1967—a summer that held so much promise in my mind—proved worse events were possible. I was ten going on fifty-four after suffering through the divorce with Mother. I had nowhere to stay that summer because I was used to coming home from school to an empty house; I was a latchkey kid way before the term was coined. But summer was a different situation. On the weekends and sometimes in the hot evenings, I went to play with Kim, the daughter of my Mother's longtime best friend Polly. Kim taught me to play chess that summer, but being around me must have driven her crazy. Kim was mature for her age, a good artist and a horse lover. She was very serious, did not like Barbies like I did, showed no passion for my imagination. But we both loved music, and this brought us together. On Saturdays I would go with her and her older sister to a nearby skating rink called Crescent Park. We donned high-top, white-booted skates, and eventually Mother even bought me new ones and paid for me to have skating lessons. I yearned for Kim's purple yarn puffballs tied into the laces at the toe of the skates. Granny said these were frivolous and the money would be wasted, but finally Mother caved in and bought me a pair of bright red ones. This brought me so much joy.

Amid the innocent fun of what childhood should be, my first personal civil rights experience came early that summer.

Georgia's new governor, Lester Maddox,* had been voted in because he was a staunch segregationist, and he had huge ideas on how to keep the African Americans "in their place."

Mother voted for Lester Maddox. Granny never talked about her choices in an election, but she was a Democrat to her death. I can't imagine she ever cast a Republican vote. Mother voted for Governor Maddox because she believed in segregation with her whole heart. The owner of Crescent Park Skating Rink liked Lester Maddox too. He had Maddox, carrying his trademark pickaxe handle, come to speak to the kids. On Saturdays, very few parents were there. Mostly it was children. Maddox spoke of protecting us from the encroaching race war on our doorsteps. I listened to him speak, but even at ten I thought he was crazy. Maybe it was due to my somewhat more diverse life in Germany—despite my mother being a raging

---

* Lester Maddox was born into severe poverty and did not finish high school. His first serious attempt at politics was his campaign for mayor of Atlanta in 1957, running against William B. Hartsfield. He was unsuccessful. Four years later in 1961 he ran against Ivan Allen Jr., who had been encouraged to enter the race to keep Maddox from winning. In 1962, Lester Maddox entered the lieutenant governor's race and was defeated. Atlanta businesses had desegregated before the passage of the Civil Rights Act of 1964, but Maddox kept his segregationist Jim Crow Policies. On July 3, 1964, Maddox and a crowd of his supporters, complete with axe handles, forcibly turned away three black activists. A photograph of the encounter ran on the front pages of newspapers across the country. Maddox's image as a violent racist was born. This incident endeared him to many white Georgians who still believed in segregation. In 1966, Maddox stunned many in Georgia politics by winning the gubernatorial race against textile heir Bo Callaway. For more about Lester Maddox, see Justin Nystrom, "Lester Maddox, 1915–2003," April 20, 2004, *New Georgia Encyclopedia*, https://www.georgiaencyclopedia.org/articles/government-politics/lester-maddox-1915-2003.

racist. I understood what that axe handle meant. When this man finished speaking, the kids stood in line to get an autographed photo of him. Kim tried to encourage me to come get a photo, but I didn't. Somehow, I couldn't celebrate this man for anything he said. Big thinking for a child of ten.

Not long after Governor Maddox's election, the owner of the skating rink made every child there sign up for a free membership to the facility. Each person was required to have a card to get into the skating rink and adjacent swimming pool. The owner had the cards printed and hired a new person for filing and monitoring the comings and goings of hundreds of kids each Friday night, Saturday afternoon, and Saturday night.

Mother gave me my card. "Put this in your wallet and show it when you pay to get inside."

"What is this for?"

"It's a membership card. Now those blacks can't get in to skate with you. They have to be a member, and the membership is full."

The joke was on the owner of the skating rink. As far as I am aware, not one African American ever came to the establishment and attempted to skate. They didn't want anything to do with the racist owner. And, the truth be told, they were afraid and rightly so. From the 1950s through the early 1970s, men like him could do anything they wanted without ever being punished.

I think it is safe to say racism was part of my life. One hot and sticky June evening, I rode in the car with Mother, sitting in the front seat as we went on an errand. We stopped at a busy intersection. Men dressed in white flowing robes, complete with hoods, stepped into the road while the traffic light was red. One of these creepy specters came up to our car. He thrust a sheet of paper through Mother's open window.

"Why is he dressed as a ghost?" I asked.

Mother reached over and pinched the inside of my arm.

"Ouch. Why did you pinch me? I just asked why he is dressed like a ghost."

"We're having a rally at the park this Saturday night," the man said. "You should come and bring your little girl. She can learn a lot."

Mother glanced at the paper. "Thank you."

The traffic light changed to green, the ghost removed himself from the window, and Mother pressed the gas, moving through the intersection.

"Ann Swafford, you could have got us killed." Her voice shook.

"Why?" I turned around and watched the ghosts weaving in and out among people's cars.

"Those ghosts, as you call them, are the Ku Klux Klan. Do you know who they are?"

I thought her question was dumb, considering that I had just asked who they were. "No."

"They are men who make it their business to be sure everyone thinks like them. They've been known to kill people if they don't follow what they say."

"What do they believe?"

"They believe everyone should be white and that coloreds don't have a say."

I sat still beside her and remained quiet as we drove down the road. She must have thought I was fearful after her explanation. And I was, but I also thought about how she believed much of the same things. Did that make her a Klan member? She didn't think so because I could see she was visibly shaken by the encounter.

By that hot June evening when Mother and I encountered the Klan, I was disgusted with summer and ready for school to begin. Of course, this wouldn't happen until the day after Labor Day. Each morning Granny took me to a house to stay with children much younger than I was. I was the oldest at ten years old. The old woman, Mrs. Keys, was the mother of Mother's good friends, Martha and Nell. She kept two young boys who were three and a girl who was seven. Our mornings were spent in the backyard. Since I was the oldest, I watched the younger kids for Mrs. Keys. After lunch, everyone, including me, had to lie down and take a nap. No reading or watching TV. Just sleeping. This was the worst insult I could have endured. As a younger child, I had developed a hatred for naps. This feeling had not dissipated. When we got up from our nap, we were sent back outside with cream-filled cookies smeared with peanut butter on the top. It was safe to say I hated summer. In the meantime, my friend Kim, who lived down the road, stayed home with her mother. She had the most fun. Many days Aunt Polly loaded her daughters into her big Oldsmobile and took them swimming. Only once had I been swimming. Granny thought it a waste of time. After the terrible sunburn she had suffered, Mother had no desire for Jeff and me to swim. Jeff spent his summer at daycare, where he seemed happy enough. At least there were all kinds of kids his age.

Around this time, I felt extremely sorry for myself and begged to stay home alone. That's when Granny came up with a great idea. She felt I needed something to keep me busy, something to challenge me.

One evening she announced that I would be going to my

Uncle Clyde's house in the country for a week. We hadn't visited him often, so I barely knew him. But this didn't keep me from being totally happy. I bragged to Kim about my upcoming trip. Excitement kept me awake several nights before we climbed into Granny's car and left on a Sunday.

"His granddaughter will be staying too," Granny announced. "She is about your age."

Mother looked over the seat at me. "You have to be on your best behavior. Clyde will need help. He hasn't looked after girls in a long time. No sassing, and respect your elders."

"I will, I promise." At the time, I loved Barbies—I made up long dramas with them, a sign of a budding writer. I also adored books and music, especially Bobby Sherman. I brought a little of all my loves with me. I had big plans.

I remember my uncle's house to this day: a white box with a large plate-glass picture window almost dead center. It sat on a hill with a steep driveway and was painted white with dark green trim. To the left of the house was a barbed-wire fence with horses watching us get out of the car.

It has been fifty years since I saw Uncle Clyde's face, and I don't remember his features. I do remember his wire-framed glasses, his large pot belly that hung over his belt, the white tank-top undershirt he wore that day, his too-pale skin. He was half bald, with only a ring of hair from ear to ear just like Arthur.

I wore a light cotton dress and so did the granddaughter, whom I will call Debbie. All girls wore dresses when they were away from home. I had on brand new navy blue Ked tennis shoes. I don't remember Mother, Jeff, and Granny leaving. Uncle Clyde sent us girls to the garden to choose a melon to go with our lunch. A warm thrill pushed through me, as if my new summer adventure would prove better than any of my friends would have.

There was a small, outdated kitchen with a refrigerator from the early fifties. Squeezed into the center of the room was a chrome table with a bluish Formica top. I scored points from the beginning by helping Clyde read the label on a food box.

"I didn't learn to read good with I was little," he admitted.

This was odd to me. Never in my life had I met an adult who couldn't read. My week of adventure was turning out just as I wanted. We sat down to the table and ate vegetables straight from the garden. Dessert was the honeydew melon chosen by us girls. I was happier than I could have ever imagined. Finally, things were going well.

Stone 29
Recurring Nightmare

We all have a moment, a particular event—whether it be a tragedy or celebration—that marks a life change, a switch, a movement, sometimes as soft as a breeze on a June morning and other times as powerful as an F5 tornado barreling through a mobile home park. This stone is the heaviest and largest in my sack, and not many days go by when I don't feel the weight cutting into my neck, straining my shoulders. The effects are at times invisible, attacking me under the skin; at other times, what happened is tattooed across my forehead. This selfish act of evil helped form who I am today. It is the elephant in the room each time I'm asked what made me use words as my art, because I was bound to be an artist, had to be, was born to be. This is the elephant I don't point out or look at unless I am pressed to notice the havoc wreaked on my life. Most of the time I pretend this elephant is nonexistent. And while I often say I began to write while listening to my grandmother and great-aunts tell stories—which is true—I don't believe I would have picked up a pen or turned on a computer to write if not for my yearning to find answers where there weren't any. Still I searched. And still I search today.

Clyde Henry Hawkins was born on February 10, 1904, and was older than Inas by five years. He was the only one of his siblings to carry his father's name. In August 1920, sixteen-year-old Clyde married Etha Lillian Carter, who was also sixteen. In 1923 the couple had their first child, Charlie Hawkins. In 1925 Grady was born. There are old photos of Jeanette and Grady hanging out together when she was sixteen and seventeen. He would have been in his early twenties at that time. Clyde and Etha had their first girl, Grace, in 1929 close to Jeanette's birthday. The couple went on to have eight children, five sons and three daughters. The 1940 census shows the youngest child being a one-year-old son. This means Etha had her last child when she was thirty-five, not old by today's standards but much older than most women had children at that time in history. Both the 1930 and 1940 census show that Clyde never attended school. In 1940 the couple lived on Nesbit Road on a rented farm.

Family lore tells that Clyde was known far and wide for beating his children unmercifully. He was known to be as mean as his father, Henry Lee.

I had no knowledge of his meanness when I went to his home that summer in 1967. He seemed to be a kind old man. He was only sixty-three years old. Etha had been dead for four years. The sixties were an innocent time, and no one would have thought it unusual for a great-niece to visit her great-uncle on his farm. And if someone did question the arrangement, he or she would not have expressed such thoughts because the code of silence in the area was thick, something left over from the generation before.

The fact that I hated to spend the night away from home filled me with sheer dread as the light seeped from the June sky. At least I had Debbie to spend the night too. This should have helped me, but around nine o'clock Uncle Clyde ordered me to bed while Debbie waited in the dining room. I stayed awake, hoping for her to come to the room, but finally I drifted off to sleep. The next morning, I was thrilled that I had slept through the night without wanting to call Mother to come get me. Even though I was an early riser, Debbie had beat me to the kitchen for breakfast. She didn't speak to me and didn't eat a bite of food. I wondered why she was mad. Less than an hour later, her father came to get her. She would not be staying the week with me.

I don't remember having one uncomfortable feeling about staying alone after she left. The day went smoothly, and I talked to Mother and Granny on the phone. Or at least, I have to assume I did. The memory isn't there, but I know Mother would have called. The memory that comes washing over me is the color pink, the same pink on our walls at home. This was the color of Uncle Clyde's bathroom. The tub, toilet, tiles on the floor and walls, and curtains on the window. I changed into my pajamas while the evening was still bright. Clyde had suggested I get ready for bed. Summer nights could stay light forever. Had we eaten dinner? I don't know. My mind is empty to any detail other than the bathroom decor and my brand new baby doll pajamas like the teenagers were wearing at sleepovers. Now I would question this sleeping attire given to a niece staying alone with her great-uncle. I didn't even have a robe. The pajamas were covered with little pink rosebuds trimmed with lace, even on the matching panties. But I trusted the visit to Uncle Clyde's. I trusted him, even if he was a little weird. I trusted Granny. I trusted everyone but Mother, who had her nervous spells and might act out at any moment. I was a young girl in love with the world, in love with my dreams of being a writer.

When I finished changing, I went into the den.

"What do you want to watch on TV?" Uncle Clyde asked. His voice was normal.

"*Batman*," I answered. My favorite show.

"Sit over here." He patted an ottoman next to where he reclined on the sofa.

Like any little girl raised by a Southern mother and grandmother during the sixties, I knew to obey my elders and treat them with respect. I sat. When he placed his hand on my leg, I remained still. I don't remember his hand moving down my leg, only his fingers invading the lacy edges of my panties. I giggled. This memory still sickens me. I giggled. Wild, scattered thoughts whirled around the room, hitting me in the chest. Maybe I would die. But I giggled.

"If you tell your mother, she will think you are a bad girl. She will hate you."

A black curtain drops on what happened. To this day, I don't know. My next memory is being told I had to sleep in the bed with him instead of alone in the guest room. Being told I was to place my arm around his waist and sleep this way. No more memories exist of what occurred. It's as if those hours of the night evaporated from the earth. Did I sleep? I find it hard to believe I did. I've been told by mental health professionals that I don't ever have to remember. I am allowed to live in the bliss of unknowing. But it doesn't work like that. Not for me. I'm too much of a thinker, a head person.

I woke up in bed the next morning with the sun streaming into the room. I usually never slept so late. I got out of the big old-fashioned bed and looked out the window. The windows were covered with thick bushes allowed to grow too tall. I hurried to the guest room and got my clothes and dressed. I packed my little blue suitcase. I had no idea how I would go home, but

I would if I had to walk. And I was a good thirty-five miles away. It was Tuesday, Granny's day off. Maybe she would come get me. I don't remember eating breakfast or lunch. I don't remember talking. Instead, I watched the sky and the clock. I only knew I could not be in that house when the sun began to go down.

At four o'clock, Aunt Polly—Mother's best friend—drove her big Oldsmobile up the driveway and parked next to the barbed-wire fence that contained the horses. A black thundercloud was blowing in from the west. She had come to buy fresh vegetables from Uncle Clyde's garden. Hope surged through me. She was strong and would save me. I busted out the screen door and met her as she emerged from the car.

"I need to go home with you. I can't stay here."

She opened her mouth, but something on my face must have stopped her. "I can't just take you home, Ann. I have to have permission from your mama or grandmother."

"Please don't leave me. Please. I'll go call." I ran in the house and used the phone in front of the big picture window in the living room. Polly went to pick vegetables. I dialed the numbers on the black rotary phone over and over and over. Granny was not at work. Where was she? The phone rang and rang.

Polly stood in the front yard.

Again, I ran out to meet her. "Please don't leave me. I have to go home."

"I can't just take you home if they are not there. Just keep trying to call them. I will go by your grandmother's on the way home and leave a note."

Tears eased out of my eyes.

"You have to be a big girl. Staying away from home is

scary."

My mind roared but I stayed quiet.

Long after she left me standing in the yard, the rain began to fall. I went inside and stood by the phone and dialed. If Uncle Clyde was around me, I don't remember. I just dialed and dialed. Finally Granny answered.

"I need to come home now," I screamed into the phone.

She sighed with irritation. "Ann, a limb from the crabapple tree has fallen across the driveway behind the car. I can't come get you right now. You'll have to stay tonight."

"No! I have to come home."

"You'll have to wait on your mother to get off from work." She sounded tired of dealing with me.

I hung up the phone and called Mother at work. Why I didn't do this to begin with speaks volumes about Granny's role as head of the house. When Mother answered her work line, she sounded professional.

"I need to come home now," I cried.

She was quiet for a minute. "Oh sweetie, I'll be there as soon as I can. You know I'm on the other side of Atlanta. Don't give up on me. I have a few more calls to take."

Mother never questioned why I had to go home. I don't mean to paint her as a great parent—I've established that she wasn't—but when I was in the worst of need, she heard the tone in my voice and came for me.

I stood by the big picture window and watched. If Uncle Clyde bothered me, I don't remember. There were no goodbyes on my part. I didn't even look at him. It was as if I had killed him off in my mind, like he never existed. When I was finally safe in the car, I watched the profile of Mother's face as the sun went down.

"Did you call your grandmother?" Mother asked as we worked our way over the curvy roads to home.

I don't remember how Granny acted when I came home. I only feel the relief of being in a safe place. I promised myself I would never spend the night away from home again.

The horrible stay with Clyde sat in my chest and weighed heavy on my shoulders, so heavy that I balled up in Arthur's chair several nights in a row with a pain that squeezed my breath out.

"I don't know what is wrong with her." Mother sounded worried.

"She probably ate something that disagreed with her stomach," Granny said.

Finally, after three weeks I told Granny as she sat at her big round mirror, rubbing Pond's cold cream on her face. She dropped the jar's metal lid when I told her. This was her only reaction.

"Are you sure this happened?" She didn't look at me.

My heart rattled in my chest. "Yes. I promise. Will you tell Mother? I can't. She will hate me. Will you promise to tell her?" Inside, I already doubted that the whole mess happened. I wondered if I had imagined what Clyde did.

Granny was quiet for a long time. "Yes." That was it. She never put her arm around me or cuddled me near. Nothing.

I believed she would tell Mother. She was Granny—my protector, the person who managed our lives.

Now, I can't remember Granny's old home phone number. All that dialing should have seared it into my brain, but I can't get past the first three numbers, 422. Even so, phones became a central theme in my childhood. They were a symbol of keeping safe. The large black rotary phone sitting in Granny's bedroom was proof that another world existed outside the place I was forced to live, the fortress around Mother. It reminded me of Granny talking on the phone at night to her best friend Mrs. Akins or her sister Beatrice.

That fall, I was again allowed to stay alone after school, but now I was afraid to walk home. Most days I ran. I worried that someone would follow me in a car. I no longer thought Mother's code of two rings, hang up, and call back was silly. She was keeping me safe. Mother believed there were a lot of bad people in the world and any random one could get me. I believed this too. I had proof.

While staying in the empty house each afternoon, I used my imagination. My writing career began in these hours. Storytelling blood was in my veins. I began to craft long, intricate stories of a girl—always a girl—on an adventure. Many ghosts were added to the mix. I'm not sure where my interest in ghosts came from. There were the stories my great-aunts told about encountering dead family members, but I think I was much more comfortable with the idea of spirits than real people. I would work on these stories until Mother's car came down the gravel drive. She frowned at my "pretending" and said others might think I was imagining things. I was: a whole world.

By the end of that fateful summer of 1967, I was having a recurring dream. In the dream I would dial a phone for help, and it would fall apart before or just as the call went through. Sometimes the numbers would melt away or move around. This recurring dream plagues me now, but the phones have become smartphones with shattered screens. I'm always trying to call a loved one to save me, help me. I always feel utterly alone, abandoned. In the dreams, no one ever comes.

When the next summer came, I was enrolled in Bible school and also stayed at Jeff's nursery school with other older siblings. Why didn't Mother try this before? I didn't love it, but it was better than staying with Mrs. Keys.

One Saturday at supper, Mother folded her paper towel and looked at me. "I think you should give Uncle Clyde's another try. It would be good for you to make it through thc whole week."

Pure hate for Mother surged through me. How could she want to send me back to that monster's house? Had it really happened, the horrible thing I remembered? Sometimes I found myself thinking it was all a bad dream, a nightmare.

"No. You can't make me. I won't go. I won't." I yelled so loud that Granny came into the room.

"What is all the yelling about? Don't talk to your mother that way."

Mother's face was red.

"I'm not going to Uncle Clyde's. You can't make me."

Nothing was ever mentioned about me staying at Clyde Hawkins's house again.

Later that summer, Mother took me with her one night and made me sit in the car while she went to a small, second-floor apartment in Atlanta to visit Grace Hawkins, Clyde's daughter. Mother and I had just finished our exercise class. This had been Granny's idea. It seems I had put some weight on during the school year, and Mother was steadily gaining. I sat in the dark at Grace's apartment, waiting, trying not to be afraid. When Mother came out, she held a photo. She had been crying. This would be the last time she saw her cousin and dear childhood friend. Grace died not long after that from liver complications due to alcohol abuse.

I wish I could say I was never abused again, that I somehow managed to be streetwise enough to see an abuser coming a mile away, but that is not true. Mother would date a succession of men who abused me. And she would fall deeper and deeper into her mental abyss, never noticing the transformation of her daughter into a fearful rebel.

Setting Down the Stones
Finally the Truth

In 1977, six years after Arthur's fatal heart attack at her house, Granny married JD's first cousin, Ollie, and became a Lord again. Ironically, his sons were angry that their father married her. Her reputation—some forty years later—still lingered in the area. Granny went back to live near Newtown, and Ollie died two years later of a massive stroke. Granny was allowed to live in the house, the family house, until she died. But she would not get any monetary gain from Ollie's estate.

In 1991, just before I turned thirty-three, I left my first husband of eighteen years. For the first time in my life, I was on my own, a very scary but freeing place. Granny became angry with me for leaving him. She accused me of seeing another man, as if being on my own was impossible. Hadn't she told me my whole life that I didn't need a man? None of it made sense. I tried to understand and not be mad at her. Couldn't she see how sad I had been, walking on eggshells all the time, trying to save my marriage, something that proved in vain? For the first time since my father left that Thanksgiving in 1966, I felt abandoned again, but I had to move forward. Even if she didn't understand my choice, I still knew it was the right place to land. Freedom.

Granny had to give up driving and moved back to her house on Joyner Avenue, where Mother lived. When her second retina transplant failed and the fate of her vision was dictated, she knew she would not go back to Ollie's home to live. The sons took possession. On top of all of this, my decision must have made her feel that her whole world was crashing in a fiery blaze.

Around this time, Mother asked me to dinner. I hesitated. By this time, Mother could be unpredictable and her mood could switch in a hiccup. I met her at a restaurant. She had been unexpectedly supportive about my decision to divorce. Maybe it was because of her own divorce. Maybe it was a fluke or a result of her manic mood. We gave the waitress our orders, and as we waited dead silence filled the space between us at the booth.

"Ann, why did you hate me so much?" Mother asked, staring at me. This wasn't a surprise question. She was always asking me things like this. I long ago stopped trying to explain to her how much I loved her, how I tried to please her my whole childhood and half my adult years. How her abuse, especially in my teenage years, drove a wedge between us.

Since I had become single, started a new life, my feelings revealed themselves so quickly that I couldn't pull them back and hide them, stuff them down. I was a big raw mess of emotions. I looked back at her and blurted out something I never thought I would say.

"Because you never did anything to Uncle Clyde for what he did to me."

Mother turned pale, grabbed her chest and leaned back. She was not beyond lying, but anyone would know I had caught her off guard, that I had delivered a blow to her, something she did not know.

A weight disappeared from my shoulders. "Didn't you know?" I managed.

She shook her head.

The background noise faded away, and for a few moments

there were only my thoughts processing, that little voice screaming in my head, the little girl so lonely and lost.

"Ann, I didn't know. What happened? Did he hurt you?"

Since my childhood, since my abuse, I had yearned for that tone, that caring tone, a loving concern. I never believed it would come from Mother. Tears trailed down my cheeks. I nodded.

"God. Why didn't I know?" she demanded.

The people at the table close to us looked our way.

The whole situation was sliding through my fingers. I had no control. I couldn't manage this emotion that was swallowing me whole.

"Why didn't you tell me?"

The room spun and I grabbed the edge of the table, took two deep breaths and steadied myself. "I told Granny right after it happened. She promised she would tell you. She promised." Could she have lied to me? How? How?

Mother shook her head, and her cheeks tinged pink. "She never told me. I swear. I'm not lying. I never knew." Her voice became loud, but I was past caring what others thought. "God, I tried to get you to go back. It was her idea. God, how can this be? Why didn't she tell me?" Never once did Mother question me. She believed me with her whole heart. "What happened?"

The waitress brought our food. When she was gone, I shook my head. "He sexually abused me. I can't talk about it, Mother. I get physically ill, and I don't remember a lot of what happened. I've been seeing a therapist for three years."

"Ann, I promise I didn't know. I would have called the police. He would not have gotten away with this. I didn't know he was like that. I never stayed with them. Grace, his daughter, always came to visit Audrey. I didn't know." Mother was quiet.

"I wonder if it happened to Grace. Is that why his granddaughter went home early that week?"

"Yes. I think he did the same thing to her." Up until that moment, I didn't know that's how I felt, that I knew he had hurt Debbie too. "I'm trying to get better, Mother. I want to put it behind me. The rage I feel sometimes is horrible. I don't trust men. I never will."

"I'm going to find out why your granny didn't tell me."

Fear crept under my skin. "Don't make a big deal out of this. Just let it go."

"No." She looked at me like I had lost my mind. "I can't pretend this never happened. I won't. You're my child."

Too much was happening.

After dinner, Mother promised to find out more and get back to me.

The next morning there was a knock on my apartment door. Mother stood there. In her hand was a small tape recorder. "I have it here. I know you didn't want to be around her. I understand why. I do. But you have to know that I may have done some bad things to you, but I wouldn't let anyone hurt you without paying."

"He's dead, Mother."

"Yes, but I needed the story of why I wasn't told. I am your mother. No wonder you wanted to be picked up that day." She pressed the play button.

Mother's forceful voice came in loud and clear. "Why didn't you tell me Clyde hurt Ann? She trusted you and you didn't tell me. Why? Why not, Mother?"

Granny's response was to sob.

Her sobbing didn't help my feelings one bit. I didn't want to hurt her. I didn't want her to ache over not following through on her promise to me.

"Do you want to go talk to her? Do you want to try and get the reason out of her?" Mother's eyes were bright with her clutching victory. Finally, she had proved to me that she was a good mother.

"No. Let's leave her alone. She's old. I know you didn't know, Mother. I saw the truth when I told you. No one could fake your reaction. I know you would have done something to him if you had known. It's over. I have closure. I've spent too much time being angry at the injustice of it all. Leave her alone. Okay?"

Mother nodded. "Okay. But she covered for him. Who would do that?'

"I don't know." And I didn't. My head reeled. Granny had lied to me and almost sent me back to stay with this man, her brother. Why? Had she known what a monster he was? Had he done the same thing to her when she was young? How many childhoods did he steal? How many innocent girls did he destroy?

I will never have the answers to any of those questions, so my self-love and healing have to be enough. Outside the window, a chilly wind blows through the colored leaves, dancing in the gusts. I lived through my childhood and have gone on to achieve the things I always wanted. Somehow I am managing to walk straight and tall. I have become the writer I dreamed of. I will not buckle and lose my heart to the messes in my past. I will keep moving forward and no longer drag around my bag of stones. Instead, I will set it down, taking one out only when it is healing for me to look back. There is a lot of lost time to make up.

Epilogue
Final Words, 2018

Mother and I had a difficult relationship. There were bittersweet moments when I knew, even through all the mental illness, dysfunction, and abuse, that she loved me. In September 2003, exactly ten years after Granny died, Mother died. And my world was empty. Dad had died in 1986 of lung cancer, though I am glad to say he and I had reunited in 1974 and found a way to have a father/daughter relationship.

The day after Mother was buried, something inside of me opened, cracked. No longer did I have to protect her from herself or from what others thought. She was free, and I was free to say and feel whatever I wanted. Writing with complete intention to tell our stories took over me. Within two months of Mother's death, my dream was realized. I was a published author. Seven years later, my first novel was accepted for publication with Simon & Schuster. Neither Mother nor Granny ever knew I made it as a writer.

Granny didn't live long enough to see me get remarried to Jack, a man I love deeply. She never met her great-granddaughter Ella, a beautiful, talented young woman. Granny never got to see her great-great-granddaughter and grandson, Melissa's children. Neither Mother nor Granny knew that my daughter Beth married a man who happened to be African American and had three children, two girls and a boy. When I look at my five grandchildren, I am proud of their diversity. I'm proud that I have these beautiful souls. I can't help but wonder what Henry Lee would think. He worked so hard to hate people for the color of their skin. And Mother—would she have accepted this family and how they turned out? Would she have grown past her legacy of racism? And what about Granny? Who was she, really? These questions can never be answered.

My brother Jeff and I lost touch. I walked away after Mother died, and—unknown to me—he went to prison for trafficking meth. I mourned him as much or more than I mourned Mother. He was gone from me, disappeared, devoured by a monster drug that owned his soul. There is no love like a sister's love for her younger brother. I'm not sure the brothers of the world understand this. I imagined that if I were lucky, I would come in one day and there would be a message on my voicemail, explaining Jeff had died from an overdose. In spring 2008, I arrived home, hit the button on my answering machine, and heard this: "I'm calling about Jeff Swafford. I believe he is your brother."

I hit the stop button. I couldn't hear that he was gone. I just couldn't. I stood still, my finger poised over the button for an undetermined amount of time. Finally, I said a silent prayer for strength and pressed play.

"I'm calling about Jeff Swafford. I believe he is your brother. I am his girlfriend and he doesn't know I'm calling. He has been clean for two years and is approaching his third anniversary. He won't call you because he is ashamed of how he has treated you. He thinks you don't want to see him again. But I know this can't be true because I have a brother, and I know how much I love him. Will you call him? He will be home tonight at seven."

And in that minute, I realized that God is in control. God waited patiently on a person I gave up on long ago, and helped him recover. Today, eleven years later, Jeff is still clean, and we are close.

As I close this four-year effort, I look at the pink ribbon stretching across the June sky. I'm older than Granny was when we came back to live with her. I think of her age when she met Arthur and understand that she was young, desperate, and determined to have a life. The light seeps from the sky. I broke the legacy of mental illness, abuse, racism, and hatred left behind by generations before me. I remove the invisible sack of rocks from around my neck and put them away. Life is too short to hold on to things that drain the soul. Regrets are useless. My heart is open to the future.

This book is a love letter to Mother. If I could tell her one thing, it would be this: I know you loved me the best way you knew how. For this I am thankful.

-The End-

Acknowledgments

Thanks to all the wonderful friends and family I questioned over and over about certain historical events. Thanks to my brother Jeff Swafford for giving me encouragement to finally tell this story, my truth. A very special thank-you to Marc Jolley, Director of Mercer University Press, for believing in this work even when I thought I would abandon the whole book and walk away. As always, thank you to Darlene Rogers for her early readings. A very special thanks to my playwright daughter, Ella, for all her input on the writing of this book. Thanks to Jack, my husband, for sticking out this project—it's finally finished!—and for the map of Forsyth County. Thanks to Melissa and Cassey for reading parts of this book while I was still writing. Thanks to Beth and Stephen for listening to me ramble about the past. A special thanks to my copyeditor, Kelley Land. Her art did wonders for this story.

Index